BAZOOKA BOYS!

Be Strong & Be Brave...
for the Lord your God is with you.
Deuteronomy 31:6

By
Kristie Kerr & Paula Yarnes
with
Jeff Kerr & Alan Bach

Copyright 2018 Kristie Kerr and Paula Yarnes. All Rights Reserved.

No part of this book may be reproduced, transmitted, or utilized in any form or by any means, graphic, electronic or mechanical, including photocopying, recording, taping, or by any information storage or retrieval, without the permission in writing from the publisher.

Unless otherwise indicated, all Scripture quotations are taken from the Holy Bible, New Living Translation, copyright ©1996, 2004, 2007 by Tyndale House Foundation. Used by permission of Tyndale House Publishers, Inc., Carol Stream, Illinois 60188. All rights reserved.

THE HOLY BIBLE, NEW INTERNATIONAL VERSION®, NIV® Copyright © 1973, 1978, 1984, 2011 by Biblica, Inc.™ Used by permission. All rights reserved worldwide.

Worldwide English (New Testament) (WE) ©1969, 1971, 1996, 1998 by SOON Educational Publications

Scripture taken from The Message. Copyright ©1993, 1994, 1995, 1996, 2000, 2001, 2002. Used by permission of NavPress Publishing Group.

Scripture taken from the Contemporary English Version ©1991, 1992, 1995 by American Bible Society, Used by Permission.

Scripture taken from the Common English Bible P.O. Box 801 201 Eighth Avenue South Nashville, TN 37202-0801

Scripture taken from the International Standard Version Release 2.1. Copyright ©1996–2012 the ISV Foundation. All rights reserved internationally.

Scripture taken from the Holy Bible, NEW INTERNATIONAL READER'S VERSION®. Copyright © 1996, 1998 Biblica. All rights reserved throughout the world. Used by permission of Biblica.

ISBN: 978-0-9970676-5-1

Printed in the United States of America

1st Printing

CONTENTS

How to Use This Book vii

What is Self-Control? 1-25
    Large Group Lesson 2
    Bible Blitz 11
    Bazooka Project 13
    Team Huddle 15
    Parent Connection 16
    Doodle Page 17
    Take Home Activity Pages
        Kindergarten – 1st Grade 19
        2nd – 3rd Grade 21
        4th – 5th Grade 23

Good Fruit / Bad Fruit 26-47
    Large Group Lesson 28
    Bible Blitz 35
    Bazooka Project 37
    Team Huddle 39
    Parent Connection 40
    Doodle Page 41
    Take Home Activity Pages
        Kindergarten – 1st Grade 43
        2nd – 3rd Grade 45
        4th – 5th Grade 47

Mind Control 50-79
    Large Group Lesson 52
    Bible Blitz 59
    Bazooka Project 61
    Team Huddle 63
    Parent Connection 64
    Doodle Page 65
    Take Home Activity Pages
        Kindergarten – 1st Grade 67
        2nd – 3rd Grade 71
        4th – 5th Grade 75

Watch Your Mouth 80-107
    Large Group Lesson 82
    Bible Blitz 91
    Bazooka Project 93
    Team Huddle 95
    Parent Connection 96
    Doodle Page 97
    Take Home Activity Pages
        Kindergarten – 1st Grade 99
        2nd – 3rd Grade 101
        4th – 5th Grade 105

Money Matters 108-131
    Large Group Lesson 108
    Bible Blitz 117
    Bazooka Project 119
    Team Huddle 121
    Parent Connection 122
    Doodle Page 123
    Take Home Activity Pages
        Kindergarten – 1st Grade 125
        2nd – 3rd Grade 127
        4th – 5th Grade 129

Using My Gifts 132-161
    Large Group Lesson 134
    Bible Blitz 143
    Bazooka Project 145

Team Huddle. 149
　　Parent Connection 150
　　Doodle Page 151
　　Take Home Activity Pages
　　　　Kindergarten – 1st Grade 153
　　　　2nd – 3rd Grade 155
　　　　4th – 5th Grade 159

Taking My Time 162-187
　　Large Group Lesson 164
　　Bible Blitz 171
　　Bazooka Project 173
　　Team Huddle. 175
　　Parent Connection 176
　　Doodle Page 177
　　Take Home Activity Pages
　　　　Kindergarten – 1st Grade 179
　　　　2nd – 3rd Grade 181
　　　　4th – 5th Grade 185

The Way to Obey. 188-215
　　Large Group Lesson 190
　　Bible Blitz 197
　　Bazooka Project 199
　　Team Huddle. 201
　　Parent Connection 202
　　Doodle Page 203
　　Take Home Activity Pages
　　　　Kindergarten – 1st Grade 205
　　　　2nd – 3rd Grade 209
　　　　4th – 5th Grade 213

Your Body, God's House 216-237
　　Large Group Lesson 218
　　Bible Blitz 223
　　Bazooka Project 225
　　Team Huddle. 227
　　Parent Connection 228
　　Doodle Page 229
　　Take Home Activity Pages
　　　　Kindergarten – 1st Grade 231
　　　　2nd – 3rd Grade 233
　　　　4th – 5th Grade 235

Hands and Feet 238-259
　　Large Group Lesson 240
　　Bible Blitz 245
　　Bazooka Project 247
　　Team Huddle. 249
　　Parent Connection 250
　　Doodle Page 251
　　Take Home Activity Pages
　　　　Kindergarten – 1st Grade 253
　　　　2nd – 3rd Grade 255
　　　　4th – 5th Grade 257

Dedicated to the boys who inspire us:

To Charlie whose tender heart and quiet spirit
remind us that **STRENGTH ISN'T ALWAYS LOUD**.

To Hunter who is **TENACIOUS AND KIND**...
and came up with the name Bazooka Boys.

To Chase who **LOVES UNCONDITIONALLY**.

To Reed who lit his homework on fire...
and then became an **HONOR STUDENT**.

To Jacob, the boy with the sensitive heart,
that captures people with his **LOVE FOR JUSTICE AND ALL THINGS SILLY**.

To Levi whose **DETERMINATION COULD DEMOLISH MOUNTAINS**
& smile could melt away the debris

To Zach who is a **TRUSTWORTHY, CONFIDENT, KIND-HEARTED** young man,
and NEVER forgets to kiss his mom goodnight!

To Li who is **KIND AND LOVING** and **ALWAYS** follows the rules!

To Stewart. The **TWINKLE IN YOUR EYE** and the tenderness in your heart
remind us that God really does make dreams come true.

You amaze us.
Go change the world.

Bazooka Boys ★ Who Am I?

HOW TO USE THIS BOOK

It seems easy enough, right? Like you really shouldn't need a page just to tell you how to use this book. And yet, here we are. We are nothing if we're not efficient!

Ok. This resource was written as a tool for use in a large group, small group or even for your family. Obviously, your specific needs may vary according to the size and make up of your group, but we have hopefully provided you with enough options that you have plenty of… well, options.

One component that we hope will help you immensely is our "Bazooka Blast Overview" located at the beginning of each chapter. This is a one page synopsis of each week's lesson. Our male co-authors have assured us that male leaders prefer fewer words than our Polka Dot Girls leaders (huh… who knew?)… so we've given you the option of "just the facts."

Each chapter starts with a large group lesson. This is something that can be taught by one teacher or even a variety of leaders. These lessons are designed to appeal to all age groups – so bring all your boys together for this part of the night. There are illustrations provided, but feel free to add in your own thoughts, insights and stories! The boys will love to hear about your own personal experiences and perspective.

***Note:** if you don't have enough space or leaders to divide your boys and girls, the Polka Dot Girls and Bazooka Boys large group lessons can be taught together. The main points of the large group lesson are usually the same – and can be adapted to teach both genders. Then consider breaking up the boys and girls into gender specific groups for small group and activity time or simply provide the Polka Dot Girls activities for the girls and the Bazooka Boys activities for the boys!

Following the large group time, we have put together a section called Bazooka Blitz which includes fun activites and games to reinforce what was learned in the lesson. We know that boys learn best while actively engaged, so we've created elements that combine scripture exploration with fun games. Boys love competition. They want to know who is the strongest, fastest and smartest. Use competition to encourage participation in small group discussion & activities. There should always be a winner. Boys won't want to participate in a competition if no one wins. Life is full of successes and failures and learning how to handle them is an important life skill.

Then it's project time! We know that some groups like to do a long term project such as creating Pinewood Derby cars – but if you want something different, we've included boy-approved and "as masculine as we can possibly make a craft" activities. Make sure you do adequate preparation depending on the age and skill level of your boys. Nothing is more frustrating than running out of time because you spent too much time cutting things out or waiting for glue to dry. (By the way… glue dries REALLY slow. Even slower when you want it to dry fast. Just our experience anyway…)

After your project time, it's time for our favorite part of the night: Team Huddle Time. This is a time to have some discussion and connection with the boys.

Huddle Time is broken down like this:

Ask This: Discussion Questions

Within each lesson you will find 3 discussion questions. We've made them short and sweet. Encourage the boys to share their stories and help them draw parallels between the spiritual truths they've learned this week and their everyday-real life situations.

Repeat This: Bible Review

Have the boys repeat the theme verse for the week. Try repeating it a few times or even let them practice individually. And we would not be opposed to some sort of "sugary reward" for those who learn it. Anything to get them to learn God's Word!

Pray This: Prayer Time

This is a great time to find out what's going on in the boy's lives. Take prayer requests and spend time praying for their needs. Challenge the boys to pray for one another and then follow up next week and see how God has answered their prayers.

Doodle This: Journal Time

Use the "Doddle This" template page (or find the corresponding page in the workbooks if the boys have purchased them separately) to have the boys explore the topics in a more personal way. Many boys are not highly verbal. They may communicate or learn better by drawing. If you don't have time, feel free to send it home and encourage them to spend some time working on it during the week.

Lastly, we've included some pages to be photocopied and sent home. They include age appropriate activity sheets and a parent partner. These are intended to give the boys some fun tools to work on throughout the week and to let the parents see what their sons are learning.

And the MOST important thing to remember is to MAKE IT WORK FOR YOU. Every group is unique and different, so feel free to add, subtract, edit, rewrite, and rework anything you find here. Find out what works and stick with it and don't be afraid to chuck the stuff that isn't working.

Our job is simple—but it couldn't be more important. We get the amazing privilege of teaching these boys about Jesus. We pray the material gives you practical tools to do just that. But above and beyond all that, remember that your gift of time and interest in these boys' lives will impact them far greater than any lesson or illustration. You are literally demonstrating for them what it means to be a man who loves Jesus. Be patient. Be loving. Be strong. Be fun. Be there.

We wish you all the best as you teach your boys what it means to be a Bazooka Boy!

BAZOOKA BLAST OVERVIEW: WEEK 1

Large Group Lesson: *(15 minutes)*

- We all have a tug of war going on in us that makes us struggle between doing the right thing and doing the wrong thing.
- Ask God to help you with self-control!
- Train yourself to be disciplined. If you can discipline yourself in the small things, you'll be disciplined in big things too!

Bazooka Blitz: Small Group Time:

Bible Blitz *(10 minutes)*
  Bible Boot Camp (Simon Says) *(Instructions on page 11)*

Bazooka Project *(20 minutes)*
  Prayerchutes *(Instructions on page 13)*

Team Huddle *(10 minutes)*

<u>Ask This:</u>

1. Have you ever decided you were **NEVER** going to do something again, and yet did it anyway? Or maybe there is something you decided you were **GOING** to do every day like practicing your piano or being nice to your brother, and yet you found yourself **NOT** doing that thing? Share your story with the group.

2. In Romans 7, Paul talks about wanting to do the right thing, but something inside pulls at him to do the wrong thing instead. Do you remember what Paul said is pulling at him? *(Answer: Our sinful nature)* Romans 7 also tells us that only one thing is stronger than our sinful nature? Do you remember what that is? *(Answer: Jesus!)*

3. What are some ways you can train yourself to be more self-controlled?

<u>Repeat This:</u> *"So think clearly and exercise self-control."* –1 Peter 1:13 NLT

<u>Pray This:</u> *"Dear Jesus, I want to do the right thing, but sometimes I find myself doing the wrong thing instead. Help me to train myself to overcome my sinful nature and become more self-controlled. Amen."*

<u>Doodle This:</u> Have the boys turn to the Doodle page in their workbook (or copy it for them).

Bazooka Boys ★ Who Am I?

WHAT IS SELF-CONTROL?

What's the Point?
God wants to help me control myself.

THEME VERSE:
So think clearly and exercise self-control.
1 Peter 1:13

RELATED BIBLE PASSAGE:
Romans 7:15–25

★ LARGE GROUP LESSON ★
(15 minutes)

When I was young, I would make the same New Year's resolution every single year without fail. I would sit in my room on December 31 and decide—with everything in my being—that this would be the year that I would reach my goal. I would be victorious! I would be a conqueror! I would do it!

What was this amazing goal, you ask?

Well, every year, I would resolve that I would not do anything wrong for an entire year.

Yup, you heard me right. No talking back to my parents. No sneaking a cookie after my mom told me I couldn't have one. No fighting with my sister. No talking in class when I wasn't supposed to. No getting into trouble.

You can imagine how far I got into the year before I blew it. Usually until about 9:38 a.m. on January 1. If I lasted even that long.

I would get so disappointed in myself. Why couldn't I do it? Why couldn't I stay out of trouble for at least one measly little day? In my heart, I so desperately wanted to do the right thing all the time, but I found that something inside of me always seemed to take over and I found myself making a bad choice once again.

Have you ever had that happen to you? You know that you shouldn't disobey your parents…you actually really want to honor your mom and dad, yet you find yourself doing the very thing they told you not to do.

Maybe you promise yourself that you're going to stop talking about your friends when they're not around, but then all your other friends start gossiping and you find yourself going along with what everyone else is doing. You leave the

Bazooka Boys ★ Who Am I?

conversation wondering, how did that happen!? I was so sure I was going to do better this time!

Or maybe you're really trying to not put off your homework so much. You come home from school determined to get your work done right away. But then you turn on the TV or start playing on the computer. Before you know it, your mom is upset with you once again because you forgot to get your homework done. Again.

Why does this happen? How can we be SO determined to do the right thing, and then find ourselves failing over and over again?

I asked God this question a few years ago. I was really frustrated with myself because no matter how hard I tried, I kept stumbling into the same mistakes over and over again. I really wanted to do the right thing, but something inside of me seemed to fight against it.

And God began to show me that I was making these same mistakes because I wasn't practicing self-control.

SELF-CONTROL...MEANS...WELL... CONTROLLING YOURSELF!

It means **MAKING** yourself do the right thing at the right time.

I think a lot of you are like me. A lot of my areas of weakness and frustration are directly linked to the fact that I don't control myself. I know the right thing, but I don't do it. I pause and say, "Oh, I shouldn't," but then I go ahead and do it anyway. Or even worse, I don't even realize I'm not practicing self-control!

I just don't pay attention. I'm acting without thinking. I'm not stopping to make sure I make good choices.

That—I am beginning to realize—is a dangerous road to be on. These might seem like small little things, but let's be honest: if we cannot control ourselves in the small things, why do we think we can control ourselves in the big things?

I recently read an article about a woman who made a really bad choice that caused a lot of people a whole lot of pain. She said, "I never once thought what I was doing was okay, but I just didn't want to stop."

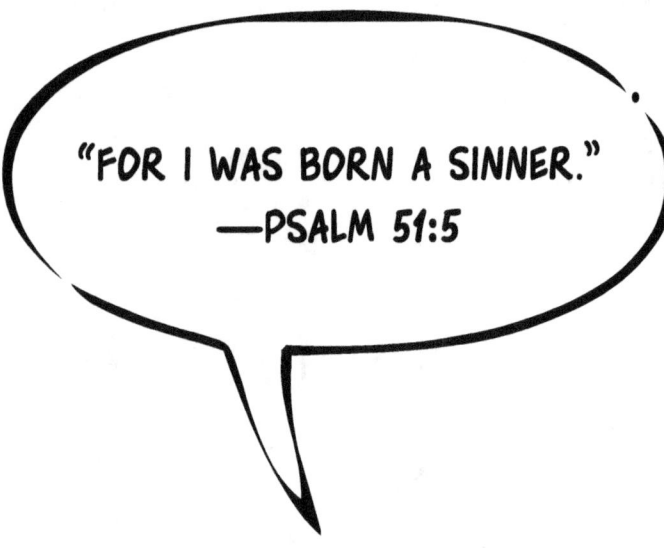

Wow. Knowing what we should do and not doing it. Facing the choices of right and wrong and not having the self-control to choose the right thing even when your heart and body and mind are telling you to do the wrong thing. This "self-control" stuff is a big, big deal.

I had a friend who used to say, "Sin is saying, 'I'm going to have what I want, when I want it.'" You may have never thought about disobeying your parents as sin, but that's exactly what it is. Sin. Saying, "I know that I shouldn't do this, but I'm going to do it anyway"—no matter how big or how small the issue may be—is a sure sign of a sinful heart.

The Bible tells us we're all born with a sinful nature. There's something inside of us that doesn't want to do the right thing! King David wrote in Psalm 51:5, "*For I was born a sinner*" (NLT). You don't have to teach a two-year-old to hit his friend upside the head when he wants to take his toy—it comes naturally because he has a sinful nature, just like the rest of us.

EVEN THOUGH YOU AND I WANT TO DO THE RIGHT THING, THERE ALWAYS SEEMS TO BE SOMETHING PULLING AT US THAT MAKES US WANT TO DO THE WRONG THING INSTEAD.

Bazooka Boys ★ Who Am I?

> **Possible Illustration:** Pick 3 volunteers
>
> One boy stands in the middle, and each of the other boys takes one of his arms. Say this: "The boy on the right represents our sinful nature. (Have him give his best "sinful nature" face.) Then the boy on the left represents our desire to do the right thing. (Have him make his best "good boy" face.)

"Let's say his Mom has asked him to pick up his room, but he REALLY wants to finish watching a show on TV. His Mom keeps asking him—and telling him—to go right now.

"(Have each boy pull on his arm—gently, of course!—back and forth like each is trying to get him to go their way.) He wants to do the right thing, but something inside him keeps telling him to stay right there on the couch, even though he **KNOWS** he should get up and help. He starts to get up (pull to the good side) but then he decides he will just wait another minute (pull to the bad side).

His Mom reminds him again, and he snaps back into reality and jumps up to go (pull to the good side)…and then he sees something funny on the screen and sits back down again (pull to the bad side). Back and forth, back and forth. He knows what he should do, but he just can't seem to do it!

Paul talks about this very thing in Romans 7:

"And I know that nothing good lives in me, that is, in my sinful nature. I want to do what is right, but I can't. I want to do what is good, but I don't. I don't want to do what is wrong, but I do it anyway (vs. 18–19)."

Can anyone relate to our buddy, Paul? He's describing in detail what it means to not have self-control. Deep in his heart, he wants to do the right things, but he feels the war within him. The things he wants to do, he doesn't do. And the things he doesn't want to do, he finds himself doing. Let's keep reading…

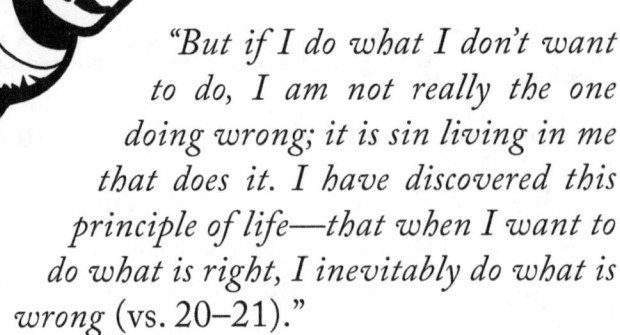

"But if I do what I don't want to do, I am not really the one doing wrong; it is sin living in me that does it. I have discovered this principle of life—that when I want to do what is right, I inevitably do what is wrong (vs. 20–21)."

Paul is telling us that no matter how hard we really want to do the right thing, the sinful nature inside of us will always be fighting against us. Now does this mean that whenever you do something wrong, you can simply say, "Sorry Mom, my sinful nature made me do it"? You can give it a try, but I don't think she's going to buy it!

BUT, it can still be helpful to realize that there's really something going on inside us that makes it hard to do the right thing.

I used to get pretty discouraged and upset with myself when I couldn't make my New Year's Resolution happen. I would beat myself up and wonder what was wrong with me. Paul shows this same frustration in Romans 7 when he says,

"Oh what a miserable person I am! Who will free me from this life that is dominated by sin and death? (vs. 24)."

So what are we to do about this? How can we learn to do the right thing at the right time? How do we learn the art of self-control?

 **1. ASK GOD TO HELP.**

If you were to read a book on self-control, you would find a lot of talk about willpower and motivation and working really hard to meet your goal. I'm not saying those things are bad—you're definitely going to need a healthy dose of

each of those things in order to live a self-controlled life. But if we believe what Paul is saying in Romans, then we should realize that not having self-control is a spiritual problem. There's sin at work in our hearts, which causes us to struggle with doing the right thing.

BOTTOM LINE: YOU CAN'T DO IT BY YOURSELF.

Without Jesus, we're powerless against sin. Our sinful nature is strong, and there's only one thing stronger: Jesus.

Romans 7:24–25 says, *"Who will free me from this life that is dominated by sin and death? Thank God! The answer is in Jesus Christ our Lord."*

Yes, your sinful nature is strong. But Jesus is stronger! Yes, it can be hard to fight to do the right thing. But Jesus has promised to help you!

When we ask Jesus to come into our lives, He comes and lives inside of us and helps us do the right thing. He has broken the power of sin in us, and if we choose to let Him, He will give us the strength to do the right thing. His Holy Spirit fills us with power, and we're suddenly able to conquer those areas of our lives that we used to think would always beat us. Jesus is stronger than our sinful nature.

As we talk about self-control in this Bible study, I know there will be times where you feel discouraged and think you just have to TRY harder. I want to encourage you, in those moments when you feel weak, remember that Jesus is the source of your strength! Ask Him to help you and believe that He will help you control yourself.

 ## 2. TRAIN YOURSELF TO BE DISCIPLINED.

First Corinthians 9:27 says, *"I discipline my body like an athlete, training it to do what it should."*

Calvin loves to play soccer. He's been playing since he was really little, and every year he gets better and better. But this year, he has a new coach who's pushing

KA-BOOM!!!

him harder than anyone ever has before. During practice, he makes the team do drills over and over again. They would practice kicking the ball back and forth, back and forth over and over and over again until Calvin wanted to scream.

Finally, one day he asked his coach, "Why do we practice the same drill so much?" He said, "We practice over and over again because during the game, it's so easy to become distracted by the crowd, the other team, and even your own emotions. When you practice the same drill over and over again, your mind will automatically know what to do in the heat of the moment because you have trained yourself. It prepares you for the moment of truth when you need to rely on what you've learned, even when it's challenging."

It's the same way with **EVERYTHING** in life! The more you practice, the easier it is to remember what you're supposed to do. The more you practice your math flashcards, the easier it is to remember your math facts. The more you practice your piano lesson, the easier it is for you to play through the songs you're learning. The more you practice riding that new skateboard, the less likely you are to fall on your booty!

Training ourselves to be self-controlled is so important. That means that we have to make ourselves do the right thing even when we don't feel like it. We choose to get up off the couch and help our mom with the dishes the first time she asks us. We pick the apple off the snack cart even though we REALLY want the cookie because we know the apple is better for us. We tell our sinful nature "**NO**" and control ourselves!

You know why it's so important to train yourself to be self-controlled in the everyday things?

Because the self-control I use when I help my mom with the dishes is the same self-control I use when I say "no" to the friend asking me to cheat on a test. The

Bazooka Boys ★ Who Am I?

self-control I use when I pick an apple is the same self-control I use when I don't steal that video game I really, really want but can't afford. The self-control that makes us choose the right thing with the little stuff is the same self-control that will help us choose the right thing with the big stuff.

1 Timothy 4:8 says, *"Physical training is good, but training for godliness is much better, promising benefits in this life and in the life to come."* I love how the Message version translates this same verse: *"Exercise daily in God—no spiritual flabbiness, please! Workouts in the gymnasium are useful, but a disciplined life in God is far more so, making you fit both today and forever."*

You need to train yourself to be self-controlled. Do something to work toward discipline. Practice saying "no" to your sinful nature. Challenge yourself in the small things so you will know how to discipline yourself in the big things.

The bottom line is this: Self-control is simply listening to what God tells you to do—and then doing it.

PRETTY SIMPLE, RIGHT?

Well, it may be simple, but simple doesn't necessarily mean easy. Let's trust God to help us be disciplined and self-controlled in every area of our lives. Jesus has promised to help us, so let's do it!

Bazooka Boys ★ Who Am I?

BIBLE BOOTCAMP (SIMON SAYS)

(10 minutes)

Leaders: Tell the boys that you are the Drill Sargent, and it is their job to follow your exact instructions! You must give the introduction **"SARGENT SAYS"** before each command. If you give a command without saying "Sargent Says" then anyone who moves must sit out until the next round.

Also, include the theme verse as one of the challenges. (*"So, think clearly and exercise self-control."* –1 Peter 1:13) Practice saying it together a few times before the game begins. When you give the command "Sargent says **SAY THE VERSE**" have everyone yell out the verse together! Do this a few times during the game to help the boys memorize it!

Some ideas for other commands:
- Sargent Says stand on one foot
- Sargent Says lift your left arm over your head
- Sargent Says snap your fingers
- Sargent Says jump up and down
- STOP (This is a great way to catch them without a "Sargent Says"
- Clap your hands
- Stomp your feet
- Sargent Says do a summersault
- Come up with your own!

Bazooka Boys ★ Who Am I?

WEEK 1

PRAYERCHUTES
(20 minutes)

Leaders: This project is especially fun if you can get to a balcony level to launch your prayerchutes. If not, the boys can simply throw their prayerchutes into the air!

<u>Supplies</u>

- Cone shape coffee filters (one per child)
- Army figurine (one per child)
- String (two per child about one foot long)
- Clear tape
- Crayons and markers

<u>Prep</u>

- In black marker, write verse "*So think clearly and exercise _____ _____.*" on the coffee filter—omitting the words "self-control" for the boys to fill in.
- Depending on the age of the kids, pre-tie the strings to the army figurine.

<u>Directions</u>

- Have each guy color their filter.
- Ask if they can remember the verse and have them write in "self-control".
- Open up the coffee filter.
- Tie one end of each string to the army figurine, taping the other end to the inside of the coffee filter.
- Get up to the launch point and have a group huddle, reviewing what self-control is and how we could think about it throughout the week. Say a prayer, and instruct the guys to launch their chutes when we say "Amen".

Bazooka Boys ★ Who Am I?

ASK THIS ★ REPEAT THIS ★ PRAY THIS ★ DOODLE THIS
(10 minutes)

Huddle up with your team just before you dismiss.

Ask This:

1. Have you ever decided you were **NEVER** going to do something again, and yet did it anyway? Or maybe there is something you decided you were **GOING** to do every day like practicing your piano or being nice to your brother, and yet you found yourself **NOT** doing that thing? Share your story with the group.

2. In Romans 7, Paul talks about wanting to do the right thing, but something inside of him pulls at him to do the wrong thing instead. Do you remember what Paul said is pulling at him? (*Answer: Our sinful nature*) Romans 7 also tells us that only one thing is stronger than our sinful nature? Do you remember what that is? (*Answer: Jesus!*)

3. What are some ways you can train yourself to be more self-controlled?

Repeat This:

"So think clearly and exercise self-control." –1 Peter 1:13 NLT

Pray This:

"Dear Jesus, I want to do the right thing, but sometimes I find myself doing the wrong thing instead. Help me to train myself to overcome my sinful nature and become more self-controlled. Amen."

Doodle This (optional):

Have the boys turn to the Doodle page in their workbook (or copy it for them.)

PARENT CONNECTION

Ahhh…self-control. So easy to talk about, and yet exponentially harder to practice. This study was birthed out of a season where God was challenging me on the lack of discipline in my life. It seemed like everytime I turned around, God was pointing out yet another area of my life where I was stumbling into sin. My lack of control of my time, my money, my thoughts, my tongue, and many other areas were constantly tripping me up.

I realized that it wasn't that I didn't **KNOW** the right thing to do. The problem was that in the moment that really counted, I didn't make myself make the right choice. I didn't eat the apple instead of the cookie. I didn't put back the extra things in my cart that weren't on the list. I didn't stop myself from sharing that juicy piece of gossip. And I didn't take control of my thoughts that led me to fear, worry, and fret. (The adult version of this study is called "Undisciplined", and you can purchase it at kristiekerr.com.)

Practicing self-control is not easy. But the good news is that God has promised to help us! This week in Bazooka Boys, we focused on Romans 7, where Paul laments his own struggle to do what he wants to do and stop doing what he doesn't want to do. As his frustration climaxes, he cries out, "Who will free me from this life that is dominated by sin and death? Thank God! The answer is in Jesus Christ our Lord."

We encouraged the boys to recognize that there is something at work in all of us that pulls us towards the wrong things. In those pivotal moments of decision, we can run to Jesus and ask Him to help us do the right thing.

We also talked about training ourselves to be self-controlled. It's not enough to just want to do the right thing, we have to actually practice making the right choices in those pivotal moments. We also discussed the fact that practicing self-control in the little things will teach us how to make good choices in the big things in life.

I invite you to be really involved with your son as he does this study. Gently remind him of the things he's working on. And encourage him when you see him disciplining himself and practicing self-control.

Bazooka Boys ★ Who Am I?

TAKE HOME ACTIVITY

WEEK 1

KINDERGARTEN AND 1ST GRADE

God wants to help you control yourself.

One of the ways God wants you to grow in self-control is by spending time praying and reading the Bible every day.

Draw a picture of yourself reading the Bible.

DRAW IT HERE!!!

Bazooka Boys ★ Who Am I?

TAKE HOME ACTIVITY

2ND AND 3RD GRADE

In Romans 7, Paul talks about wanting to do the right thing, but something inside of him pulls at him to do the wrong thing instead. Jesus wants us to have self-control. It's much better to think before you act.

Find your way through the maze. Remember to think before you act!

Bazooka Boys ★ Who Am I?

4TH AND 5TH GRADE

You need to train yourself to be self-controlled. Next to each letter, list something you can do to work toward self-discipline. **Remember:** Challenge yourself in the small things so you will know how to discipline yourself in the big things.

Example: S - Scripture memorization

S _____

E _____

L _____

F _____

C _____

O _____

N _____

T _____

R _____

O _____

L _____

In Romans 7, Paul describes in detail what it means to not have self-control. Deep in his heart, he wants to do the right things, but he feels the war within himself. The things he wants to do, he doesn't do. And the things he *doesn't* want to do, he finds himself doing.

Read Romans 7:15–25 in your Bible, and fill in the missing words in the verses below (all verses NIV).

v. 15 *I do not _____ what I do. For what I want to do I do not do, but what I hate I do.*

v. 16 *And if I do what I do not _____ to do, I agree that the law is good.*

v. 17 *As it is, it is no longer I myself who do it, but it is _____ living in me.*

v. 18 *For I know that _____ itself does not dwell in me, that is, in my sinful nature. For I have the desire to do what is good, but I cannot carry it out.*

v. 19 *For I do not do the good I want to do, but the _____ I do not want to do—this I keep on doing.*

v. 20 *Now if I do what I do not want to do, it is no longer I who do it, but it is sin _____ in me that does it.*

v. 21 *I find this _____ at work: Although I want to do good, evil is right there with me.*

v. 22 *For in my inner being I delight in _____ law;*

v. 23 *But I see another law at work in me, waging war against the law of my mind and making me a _____ of the law of sin at work within me.*

v. 24 *What a wretched man I am! Who will _____ me from this body that is subject to death?*

v. 25 *Thanks be to God, who _____ me through Jesus Christ our Lord! So then, I myself in my mind am a slave to God's law, but in my sinful nature a slave to the law of sin.*

Word List

Understand	*Living*	*Evil*	*God's*
Law	*Sin*	*Delivers*	*Save*
Good	*Prisoner*	*Want*	

Bazooka Boys ★ Who Am I?

WEEK 1

BAZOOKA BLAST OVERVIEW: WEEK 2

Large Group Lesson: *(15 minutes)*
- Our flesh is the selfish part of us that always wants our own way.
- We need to push down our flesh! Tell it "**NO!**"
- Then we need to fill up with the Holy Spirit.
- The Holy Spirit grows good fruit in our lives—including the fruit of self-control.

Bazooka Blitz: Small Group Time:

    Bible Blitz *(10 minutes)*
        Holy Spirit Balloon Experiment *(Instructions on page 35)*

    Bazooka Project *(20 minutes)*
        Fruit Test *(Instructions on page 37)*

    Team Huddle *(10 minutes)*

    <u>Ask This:</u>

1. What is our flesh? (*Our flesh is the part of us that wants whatever it wants whenever it wants it*) How do we push down the flesh? (*We tell our bodies who's boss, we tell ourselves NO, and we do what is right even if we don't want to*)

2. After we push down the flesh, what do we do? (*Fill up with the spirit*) What does the Holy Spirit do when we ask Him to fill us up? (*He gives us power to overcome our flesh*)

3. What kind of fruit does the Holy Spirit produce in us? (*Love, Joy, Peace, Patience, Kindness, Goodness, Faithfulness, Gentleness, Self-Control*) What kind of fruit do you think is showing the MOST in your life? What kind of fruit is showing LEAST in your life?

<u>Repeat This:</u> "*So I say, let the Holy Spirit guide your lives. Then you won't be doing what your sinful nature craves*". –Galatians 5:16

<u>Pray This:</u> "*Dear Jesus, I need you to help me do the right thing, even when I don't feel like it. Help me push down my flesh and say "NO" when I need to. Fill me with the power that comes from your Holy Spirit. I pray that my life would show good fruit to others. Amen.*"

<u>Doodle This:</u> Have the boys turn to the Doodle page in their workbook (or copy it for them).

Bazooka Boys ★ Who Am I?

GOOD FRUIT / BAD FRUIT

WHAT'S THE POINT?
I NEED TO PUSH DOWN MY FLESH AND FILL UP WITH THE HOLY SPIRIT!

THEME VERSE:

*So I say, let the Holy Spirit guide your lives.
Then you won't be doing what your sinful nature craves.*
Galatians 5:16

RELATED BIBLE PASSAGE:

Galatians 5:16–26

★ LARGE GROUP LESSON ★
(15 minutes)

"I HATE cleaning my room!"

Joseph was stomping around his room, throwing things into his closet and muttering under his breath. All his friends were outside enjoying the sunshine while he sat indoors picking up clothes off the floor.

"It's not fair," he said to himself. "All my friends get to do whatever they want. Why does my mom always make me do what **SHE** wants me to do? I just want to be able to do what I want to do!"

Have you ever had that happen to you? You REALLY want to play outside with your friends, but your parents make you do chores first? Or you REALLY want to have free time in class, but your teacher makes you do an extra assignment first? Or maybe you really want to play a certain game, but it's your friend's turn to choose and you have to play what he wants instead?

We can probably all remember a time when we didn't get what we wanted. It can be pretty frustrating.

Imagine what it would be like if you could do whatever you wanted **ALL** the time! Chocolate ice cream for breakfast, lunch, and dinner. Recess for four

Bazooka Boys ★ Who Am I?

hours a day. No homework. No chores. As much TV and computer time as you want – whenever we want it.

Sounds pretty good, doesn't it?

Well, it does sound good at first, but what happens when your stomach hurts and you get a toothache from only eating chocolate ice cream? And what happens when you grow up and you don't know how to read or do math because you had recess all day at school instead of learning the things you needed to learn? And what happens when you **NEVER** clean your room and suddenly you can't find any clean clothes to wear to school and your room starts to smell really bad because of all the stinky socks stuck in the corner? That doesn't sound like much fun either.

Sometimes we think of freedom as being able to do whatever we want. We think we should only have to do the things that are fun! We think we should be able to do things whenever we want to—instead of when our teacher or parents want us to do things. We try and avoid things that are hard and not so fun. But that isn't the way life works. Most of life is made up of doing the things that we **SHOULD** do, not the things we **WANT** to do.

You may not feel like cleaning your room, but you know it's the right thing to do. You may not feel like doing your homework, but you do it because you know it's important to learn things. You may not feel like taking turns with your friends, but you do it because you know a good friend takes turns.

ONE OF THE GREATEST WAYS THAT WE CAN PRACTICE SELF-CONTROL IS BY DOING THE THINGS WE MAY NOT WANT TO DO, BUT THEY'RE THE RIGHT THINGS TO DO.

Joseph didn't **WANT** to pick up his room, but when he choose to obey his parents and do what they asked, he was choosing what was better. He was showing honor to his parents. He was being responsible by taking care of the things he owned. He was being a good example to his friends by doing the right thing. More important than all these things, something happened inside Joseph when he decided to do the right thing, even when he didn't feel like it.

You see, something happens in us when we put aside our own feelings and do what we **SHOULD** do, even when we don't **WANT** to.

The Bible talks a lot about our **FLESH**. What in the world does "flesh" mean? Well, it's the thing inside of us that makes us only think about ourselves and what we want. It's part of the "sinful nature" we talked about last week. It's the little voice inside your head that says, "You should always get what you want." It whispers, "You shouldn't have to do anything you don't want to do." The flesh is all about me, me, me. Making ME happy. Making sure I always get to do what I want.

Ick. Our flesh is pretty yucky.

Jesus tells us over and over again that we should not let our flesh be the boss of us. We should think of others before ourselves. We should do the right thing even if it's not easy. Our flesh wants to lead us down one path, but God's path is way better!

So, how do we fight this flesh thing? How do we overcome that voice that tells us to only do what we want instead of what's right?

There's a magic formula! Ready?

 We **PUSH** down the **FLESH** and **FILL UP** with the **SPIRIT**!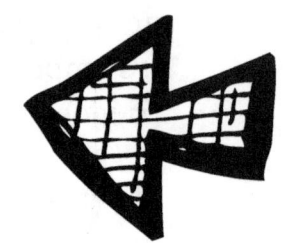

Teacher Note: As you talk through these points, use these hand gestures for emphasis and have the boys do them with you. Take both hands and make a downward motion when you say "Push down our flesh" and then do the reverse action—raising both hands back up while you say "Fill up with the Spirit."

Practice these three or four times before you explain the following points.

1. PUSH DOWN OUR FLESH.

Galatians 5:16 says, *"So I say, let the Holy Spirit guide your lives. Then you won't be doing what your sinful nature craves."*

Remember last week when we talked about the two sides pulling at us? The tug of war to do the right thing verses the tug of war to do the wrong thing? That's what this verse is talking about. Good and evil are at WAR inside us!

We have to **FIGHT** hard to help the good side win. And the more the good side wins, the stronger it becomes.

Having self-control means you push down your flesh with everything in you. You tell your mind and body and actions "**NO**!"

Illustration: Take an empty garbage can or other container. Fill it with pieces of crumpled up newspaper.

"Take a look at this garbage can. It is **FULL** of newspaper. Just like you and I can be **FULL** of our **FLESH**. But we don't have to let our flesh be the boss of us. We can push it down!"

(Push down the newspaper with your hand or foot, and maybe let the kids take a turn pushing down the paper too!)

"When we push down our flesh, we make room for the Holy Spirit to fill us up instead!"

When your flesh tells you to take that cookie even though your Mom told you not to, you push down your flesh and say, "**NO COOKIE FOR YOU**!" When your flesh tells you to share that secret about a friend that you promised you wouldn't share, you push down your flesh and say, "**NO! I'M NOT GOING TO TELL THAT SECRET**!" When your flesh tells you to cheat on the test so you can get a better grade, you push down your flesh and say, **"NO! I'M NOT GOING TO DO SOMETHING I KNOW IS WRONG!"**

First Corinthians 9:27 says, *"I keep my body under control and make it my slave..."*(CEV). Another version says, *"It is my own body I fight to make it do what I want."*(ERV) Sometimes the thing we're fighting is our very own body. Sometimes I have to smack myself upside the head and say, "No! I will not listen to you! I will not let you be the boss of me!"

Push down your flesh. Don't let it bully you into doing something you know is wrong.

So, we push down then flesh, and then we…

 ## 2. FILL UP WITH THE SPIRIT.

Micah 3:8 says, *"But me—I'm filled with God's power…"* (MSG). And Acts 1:8 says, *"But you will receive power when the Holy Spirit comes upon you"*.

When you push down that gross, yucky flesh, you make room for God's awesome and amazing power to fill you up! The Holy Spirit gives you the **POWER** to fight your flesh and have self-control!

ILLUSTRATION: (Use the same garbage can or container full of newspaper from the previous illustration. Now that the newspaper has all been pushed down, begin to fill it up with brightly colored tissue paper.)

"When you push down your flesh, you make room for the Holy Spirit in your life. Instead of being bossed around by your flesh, now the Holy Spirit is in charge. When we fill up with the Holy Spirit, all the good things the Holy Spirit brings us will start to show in our lives, including love, joy, peace, and lots of other good stuff!"

Bazooka Boys ★ Who Am I?

WEEK 2

Austin was feeling super nervous about going to school. Every morning he would begin walking toward his school and his mind would start picturing every possible bad thing that could ever happen. He worried that he would drop his tray at lunch. He wondered if his teacher would call on him when he didn't know the answer. He thought about how embarrassed he would be if he didn't have anyone to play with at recess. The more he thought about it, the more anxious and afraid he would get. His thoughts kept coming faster and faster until his heart was beating fast and he thought he might throw up.

But he remembered that he didn't have to let his thoughts boss him around, so the next time a bad thought came into his head, he pushed down his flesh and told it to go away. Over and over again, he knocked those thoughts right out of his head and told them to go away.

Austin realized that, not only did he need to get the bad thoughts out, he needed to fill up with good thoughts. He asked the Holy Spirit to come and fill his thoughts with good things instead. He prayed for the Holy Spirit's power to give him strength to fight his flesh. He remembered a verse his mom taught him that said, *"For I can do everything through Christ who gives me strength"* (Philippians 4:13), and he started saying it over and over again.

He pushed those bad thoughts out and filled his mind with the power of the Holy Spirit. Every time he pushed down the flesh, he filled the space with a reminder that God was with him and he could do anything with God's help!

The Holy Spirit will fill you with the power to overcome your flesh. He will fight it for you. When you ask Him to help you, His strength comes into you and gives you **SUPERNATURAL** power to practice self-control.

So, we push down our flesh, we fill up with the Spirit, and then we . . .

 **3. GROW SOME FRUIT.**

What kind of tree grows an apple? What kind of tree grows an orange? What kind of tree grows a lemon?

Of course an apple tree grows apples. An orange tree grows oranges. And a lemon tree grows lemons. You can tell what kind of tree it is by the kind of fruit it produces. It even says this in the Bible. Luke 6:44 says, *"A tree is identified by its fruit."*

It's the same way with our lives. The Bible says that if we really love Jesus and we're following Him, we'll see certain kinds of fruit in our lives. Galatians 5:22 says, *"But the Holy Spirit produces this kind of fruit in our lives: love, joy, peace, patience, kindness, goodness, faithfulness, gentleness, and self-control."*

If our lives belong to Jesus, the "fruit" of our lives—the things other people notice about us—should be love, joy, peace, and all the other fruits of the Spirit… including self-control!

If we push down our flesh and we fill up with the Spirit, then we'll see more and more of these things in our lives. If I'm filling myself with the Spirit, I'll be a more loving person. If I'm filling myself with the Spirit, I'll be a more patient person. If I'm filling myself with the Spirit, I'll have more self-control.

The reverse is also true, isn't it? If you're not very loving, you need more of the Spirit. If you're not very patient, you need more of the Spirit. And if your life isn't demonstrating self-control, you need more of the Spirit.

If our fruit shows a lack of peace, we need less of the flesh and more of the Spirit. If our fruit shows a lack of gentleness—we're harsh and snappy and unkind—we need less of our flesh and more of the Spirit. And if we find ourselves struggling to be disciplined, we need less of the flesh and more of the Spirit.

What is the secret to discipline? Less of the flesh and more, more, more of Jesus.

He is the answer. He is where we go to deal with our lack of discipline.

Push down the flesh, fill up with more of the Spirit, and grow good fruit.

Bazooka Boys ★ Who Am I?

HOLY SPIRIT BALLOON EXPERIMENT

(10 minutes)

Supplies

- Balloon (one per child)
- One candle
- Lighter or match

Prep

- Fill one balloon with water.

Directions

1. Have each child blow up the balloon by mouth.
2. Assist with tying.
3. Option: Have boys draw a face on the balloon with a sharpie.
4. Set up candle on table.
5. Have the leader take the balloons one at a time and put them over the flame. The flame will pop these balloons.
6. Place the water balloon over the flame to demonstrate that a balloon filled with water will not pop.

Explain that the balloon full of air represents our flesh or our selfishness. It is full of our own air, leaving no room for the Holy Spirit.

And just like the balloon full of air pops when it gets next to the flame, we will fall apart when we face temptation if we are full our flesh.

But the balloon filled with water represents the Holy Spirit! If we are full of the Holy Spirit, we have the power to resist temptation. The water balloon over the flame does not burn or pop. And if we fill ourselves up with the Holy Spirit, we will stay strong no matter what we face!

Bazooka Boys ★ Who Am I?

FRUIT TEST

(20 minutes)

Supplies

- Different kind of fruit, some easier to distinguish than others
- Paper lunch bags
- Whiteboard or blackboard

Prep

- Number bags 1-7
- Place one fruit in each bag

Directions

1. Place the seven different fruits in separate paper bags.
2. Number the bags and put the numbers on the blackboard to record responses.
3. Let each boy reach into the bag without looking and decide what they think is in the bag.
4. Write the boys responses on the blackboard.
5. Once everyone has a turn, discuss which fruits were easy and which were hard.
   a. Take a moment to talk about different temptations. Some kids find it hard to obey their parents, while others don't struggle as much with that particular issue.
   b. Example: If I don't love chocolate cake, it's easier to have self-control when mom says not to have any before dinner.
   c. Ask the boys if there is an area that is easy for them to self-control.
   d. Remind the boys that everyone struggles with different things, but we all need to have self-control.

ASK THIS ★ REPEAT THIS ★ PRAY THIS ★ DOODLE THIS
(10 minutes)

Huddle up with your team just before you dismiss.

Ask this:

1. What is our flesh? (*Our flesh is the part of us that wants whatever it wants whenever it wants it*) How do we push down the flesh? (*We tell our bodies who's boss, we tell ourselves NO, and we do what is right even if we don't want to*)

2. After we push down the flesh, what do we do? (*Fill up with the spirit*) What does the Holy Spirit do when we ask Him to fill us up? (*He gives us power to overcome our flesh*)

3. What kind of fruit does the Holy Spirit produce in us? (*Love, Joy, Peace, Patience, Kindness, Goodness, Faithfulness, Gentleness, Self-Control*) What kind of fruit do you think is showing the MOST in your life? What kind of fruit is showing LEAST in your life?

Repeat This:
"So I say, let the Holy Spirit guide your lives. Then you won't be doing what your sinful nature craves." – Galatians 5:16

Pray This:
"Dear Jesus, I need you to help me do the right thing, even when I don't feel like it. Help me push down my flesh and say "NO" when I need to. Fill me with the power that comes from your Holy Spirit. I pray that my life would show good fruit to others. Amen."

Doodle This:

Copy the Doodle page for the boys (or have them turn to that page in their workbooks).

PARENT CONNECTION

We all feel the tug of war between our flesh and the Spirit. We identify with Paul in Romans 7 when he shares the experience of desperately wanting to do the right thing, yet consistently choosing to do the very thing he didn't want to do. Our kids are no different. For the most part, they want to do the right thing—to obey us, get their homework done, and refrain from talking back. But they feel that same internal struggle we do, between what we know we **SHOULD** do and what we find ourselves actually doing.

There's hope for all of us! Even though our flesh tries to pull us to the dark side, we **KNOW** that the Holy Spirit has the power to help us fight our flesh. This week we taught the boys to fight their flesh by pushing it down when they feel it pulling at them with temptation. And after they push down their flesh, they fill themselves up with the Holy Spirit! They can make space for Him by dying to their flesh and inviting Him to come and fill us up. When they fill up with the Holy Spirit, they can watch the good fruit He promises to grow in them come to life. And if they see good fruit, they can know that the Holy Spirit is at work in their heart! Likewise, when they notice bad fruit popping up (such as a lack of self-control) they can recognize that it's time to push down that flesh again and fill up with more of the Holy Spirit.

Help your child recognize their bad fruit and teach them to rely on the Holy Spirit to grow good fruit in them every day!

Bazooka Boys ★ Who Am I?

Bazooka Boys ★ Who Am I?

 TAKE HOME ACTIVITY

KINDERGARTEN AND 1ST GRADE

Galatians 5:22–23 tells us that the fruit of the Spirit is: love, joy, peace, patience, kindness, goodness, faithfulness, gentleness, and self-control.

Write out the name of each fruit on the tree and then color in the picture!

Bazooka Boys ★ Who Am I?

 **TAKE HOME ACTIVITY**

 WEEK 2

2ND AND 3RD GRADE

Look up Galatians 5:22–23 in your Bible. Write out the nine fruits of the Spirit on the tree and then color the picture.

Bazooka Boys ★ Who Am I?

4TH AND 5TH GRADE

Look up Galatians 5 in your Bible. Verses 19–21 list 16 bad things that will show up in your life if you're letting your flesh control you. What are they?

1.
2.
3.
4.
5.
6.
7.
8.
9.
10.
11.
12.
13.
14.
15.
16.

Verse 22 tells us the good fruit that will be present in a life that is controlled by the Spirit. List those nine things here:

1.

2.

3.

4.

5.

6.

7.

8.

9.

WEEK 2

BAZOOKA BLAST OVERVIEW: WEEK 3

Large Group Lesson: *(15 minutes)*
- God wants us to have self-control with the things we think about!
- Let the Holy Spirit be the boss of your brain.
- Kick the habit of thinking negative thoughts!
- The "W" plan means we think about "whatever" is good.

Bazooka Blitz: Small Group Time:

Bible Blitz *(10 minutes)*
Kick the Can to Kick the Habit *(Instructions on page 59)*

Bazooka Project *(20 minutes)*
"Who's the Boss" Balloon Rocket *(Instructions on page 61)*

Team Huddle *(10 minutes)*

Ask This:
1. God doesn't want us thinking about negative things, scary things, bad things or things that make us worried. If you want to – share one thought that you have struggled with which left you sad, scared or nervous.

2. When do you struggle most with your thoughts? Is it bedtime? In the morning before school? When you're away from your family? What is one way you could **KICK THE HABIT** of thinking bad thoughts during those times?

3. What is the "W" plan? What are some true, lovely, pure, excellent, worthy of praise things that you can think about this week?

Repeat This: *"Fix your thoughts on what is true, and honorable, and right, and pure, and lovely, and admirable. Think about things that are excellent and worthy of praise."* –Philippians 4:8

Pray This: *"Dear Jesus, I want the Holy Spirit to control my thoughts. Help me kick the habit of thinking about things that aren't good, helpful, or pleasing to you. I want to honor you in the way I think. Amen."*

Doodle This: Have the boys turn to the Doodle page in their workbook (or copy it for them).

MIND CONTROL

What's the Point?
God wants you to think about good things, not bad things!

THEME VERSE:
Fix your thoughts on what is true, and honorable, and right, and pure, and lovely, and admirable. Think about things that are excellent and worthy of praise.
Philippians 4:8

RELATED BIBLE PASSAGE:
Romans 8

★ LARGE GROUP LESSON ★
(15 minutes)

Our brains are pretty amazing things. Some people say the average human thinks 70,000 thoughts every single day. That's a lot of thinking!

The Bible tells us Jesus knows **EVERY SINGLE THOUGHT WE HAVE!** Psalm 94:11 says, *"The Lord knows people's thoughts."* I'm not sure how I feel about that. On one hand, it's so incredible to know God understands every single thing about me without me even saying a word, but on the other hand, I wouldn't say I'm totally proud of each and every thought that crosses my mind. I'm usually happy when I don't act on a negative thought, but the Bible says that if I even think it, He knows it. Yikes! Even more reason to be amazed at God's love for me—He knows everything I think about and still loves me. Crazy!

The Bible encourages us to be careful about the things we think about. God knows how easy it is to think about things we shouldn't. We all have areas of our lives where we allow our thoughts to go places they shouldn't. And sometimes we find our train of thought stuck on a certain pattern of behavior or consumed by a certain way of thinking.

Some of us get stuck always thinking negative thoughts. We can be critical of other people—always putting them down in our minds. We can also be critical of ourselves—saying negative things to ourselves all the time like, "You're so dumb! No one likes you! You're not good at anything!" God doesn't want us to always think negative thoughts.

Maybe you've seen something you shouldn't have seen or done something you shouldn't have done, and now you can't stop thinking about something you know isn't honoring to God.

Some of us get stuck thinking about the past. You can't help but remember

Bazooka Boys ★ Who Am I?

and think about things that happened in the past. Maybe you keep thinking about a mistake you made and you replay it over and over again in your mind. It can be so easy to get stuck in the past.

Maybe your mind gets stuck in WORRY mode and your thoughts are consumed by what COULD happen. Your thoughts might even be kind of scary. Your mind seems to always think about the worst possible thing, and you have a hard time stopping it.

So, I have a question for you: why do we let our thoughts focus on such negative things?

Maybe that seems like a trick question. You might be thinking, "What do you mean I 'let' my thoughts be negative?" I don't know about you, but many times I think I don't have any control over the thoughts going through my head. They seem to just happen!

But God tells us that we should CONTROL the thoughts going through our mind. What does it mean to control something? It means you're the BOSS of it. You're in charge and it has to do whatever you tell it to do.

Remember last week when we talked about 1 Corinthians 9:27? It says, *"I keep my body under control and make it my slave..."* (CEV). Well, the most important part of your body to keep as your slave is your BRAIN. You can't just let your thoughts go wherever they want to go. Make them your slaves and tell them they have to do whatever you tell them to do!

YOU KNOW WHY THAT'S SO IMPORTANT? BECAUSE YOUR THOUGHTS EVENTUALLY BECOME YOUR ACTIONS.

You might think it's not harming anyone else to think bad things, but the truth is that whatever you're thinking about eventually comes out in the way you treat others. Most of all, it will hurt YOU. Proverbs 4:23 says, *"Above all, be careful what you think because your thoughts control your life"* (ERV). The things you think about are important.

Last week, we talked about the fruit of the Spirit: love, joy, peace, patience, kindness, goodness, faithfulness, gentleness, and self-control. This is the good fruit that should be overflowing in our lives. But you know what? Your mind is an easy place to grow **BAD** fruit.

We aren't very loving because we're filled with unloving thoughts toward other people. We're not filled with joy because our minds are focused on disappointments. Our minds aren't peaceful because we're worried about so many things. We're not patient, kind, good, faithful, or gentle in our thoughts. Instead, we're impatient, rude, harsh, disloyal, and destructive in the things we think about.

So, how can we learn to discipline our thoughts?

1. LET THE HOLY SPIRIT BE THE BOSS OF YOUR BRAIN!

Who gets to be the boss of your brain? The Holy Spirit! Romans 8:6 says, *"So letting your sinful nature control your mind leads to death. But letting the Spirit control your mind leads to life and peace."*

We need to push down the flesh that wants to fill our thoughts with negative and sinful things, and instead fill up our minds with the Holy Spirit. Invite the Holy Spirit into your thoughts. Say, "Holy Spirit, you're the boss of my brain!" When He's in charge, He will fill up your mind with all the good fruit of the Spirit and there won't be room for all that yucky, negative stuff!

Bazooka Boys ★ Who Am I?

The second way you can discipline your THOUGHTS is to...

 **2. KICK THE HABIT!**

What's a habit? It's something you do all the time without thinking about it. Some people have a habit of biting their nails or chewing with their mouth open. What habits to you have?

We all have habits—and it's no different when it comes to our thought life. It's easy to get in the habit of thinking in a certain way or constantly focusing on a certain topic. And if you want to break **ANY** habit, you have to work hard at changing your behavior. You have to **KICK THE HABIT**!

If you're in the habit of thinking of the worst things all the time, you're going to need to change that behavior. Catch yourself focusing on bad stuff. When you realize you're thinking something that isn't good, stop yourself right away and begin to think about good things instead!

Landon had a hard time falling asleep. Every night he would crawl into bed and his mind would begin to go crazy. He would imagine all kinds of scary things. He

would imagine there was something in his closet. He would imagine he was lost and couldn't find his mom. Sometimes he even imagined missing the goal in the final seconds of a championship hockey game and letting all his teammates down! He wasn't sure where all these negative thoughts came from, but they sure did bother him.

One day he realized he had gotten in the habit of thinking bad things every night at bedtime. It just got to be the way his brain decided to boss him around at night. So he decided to **KICK THE HABIT**!

When he got into bed, as soon as the first scary thought popped into his mind, he thought of something funny instead. Or he would repeat a Bible verse his mom had taught him: "*Be strong and courageous! Do not be afraid, for the Lord God is with you wherever you go* (Joshua 1:9). Every time his brain tried to take him back to a scary thought, he **KICKED** that habit right in the teeth and thought of something **GOOD** instead.

You are in control of what you think about. You have the power to simply stop thinking about things that make you sad, worried, or frustrated. Refuse to focus on those things. Kick that bad habit, and think about good stuff instead! Don't allow your thoughts to go wherever they want to. You can control what you think about.

Psalm 119:95 says, "*…I will quietly keep my mind on Your laws.*" You have the power to keep your mind fixed on the things you want to think about, like what God says is true. And you have the power to keep your mind away from the things you shouldn't be thinking about.

And the last way you can discipline your thoughts is to focus on…

 ## 3. THE "W" PLAN!

One of my all-time favorite verses in the Bible is Philippians 4:8: "*Finally, brothers and sisters, whatever is true, whatever is noble, whatever is right, whatever is pure, whatever is lovely, whatever is admirable—if anything is excellent or praiseworthy—think about such things.*"

Isn't that a great verse? It tells us to think about **"WHATEVER"** is good! And **"WHATEVER"** is true! And **"WHATEVER"** is lovely! So when I'm having a hard time controlling my thoughts, I put up three fingers to make a "W" and start using my "W" plan!

What is the "W" plan?

Well, when a thought comes knocking at the door to my brain, I pretend there's a little peep-hole to look through the door and before I answer it I say, "Are you a **WHATEVER** thought?" I'm basically asking, "Are you a good thought or a bad thought?" and "Are you a true thought or a lie?" and "Are you a lovely thought or a scary thought?" If it's not a **"WHATEVER"** thought, I don't open the door! I tell those yucky thoughts to stay outside my brain. I don't want them in there!

Now, we all have times when a bad thought sneaks into our brain. It's just part of being human. But we can decide how long we let those thoughts stick around.

ILLUSTRATION: Sieve vs. Bowl

(Have a pitcher of water, a bowl, and a sieve with a bowl underneath.)

"We all have negative thoughts come into our minds from time to time. Maybe it's a mean thought about a friend. Or maybe it's a scary thought about something bad that might happen. Or maybe it's a thought about something you know doesn't make Jesus happy. Our thoughts are like this pitcher of water."

(Pour the water into the first bowl slowly as you share the next point.)

"But the problem comes when you let that thought just sit in your mind, just like the water is sitting in this bowl. Then that thought just sits there, and stays in your mind and you keep thinking, and thinking, and thinking about it until pretty soon it's affecting your whole life."

(Slowly pour the water into the second bowl through the sieve.)

"**BUT** you can let your mind be like this sieve. When a thought comes into your mind, you can immediately recognize that it's not a **"WHATEVER"** thought and let it roll right out of your brain. This will help you keep your thoughts from getting filled up with things that aren't good for you."

You don't have to **LET** just any thought just roam around in your brain. If you let the Holy Spirit be the boss, He will help you think about love, joy, peace, and other good things! He will help you **KICK THE HABIT** of thinking about things that aren't good for you.

Colossians 3:2 says, "*Set your mind on things above, not things of earth*" (NIV). God wants your mind to be a place with lots of good fruit. He doesn't want you feeling sad, scared, angry, or negative all the time. Choose to make your brain a place full of good stuff!

KICK THE CAN TO KICK THE HABIT

(15 minutes)

Supplies

- Can/Cone/Ball—anything that can be kicked.

Prep

- Designate where the jail will be.

Directions

1. Divide the boys into teams. One team will guard the can and one team will try to kick it over.

2. The defenders try to tag the runners. If a runner is tagged, he must go to jail.

3. The goal is for the defenders to tag every runner before the can is kicked.

4. If a runner does kick the can, all the captured runners that are in the "jail" can go free.

5. Once a team wins, have everyone recite the theme verse and then switch positions!

Bazooka Boys ★ Who Am I?

"WHO'S THE BOSS" BALLOON ROCKET
(20 minutes)

Supplies

- Large balloons (one per child)
- Tape
- Straws (one per child)
- Long string (small enough to fit through the straw)
- Chair

Prep

- Tie one end of the string to the back a chair.
- Pre cut tape into 1 inch strips.

Directions

1. Blow up balloons, but don't knot them. Keep the end pinched so no air escapes.

2. Tape the straw to the inflated balloon.

3. Feed the string through the straw.

4. Pull the string tight.

5. Release the end of the balloon end and watch it fly toward the chair.

Remind the boys that Romans 8:6 tells us to let the Holy Spirit be "the boss of our brain!"

Bazooka Boys ★ Who Am I?

ASK THIS ★ REPEAT THIS ★ PRAY THIS ★ DOODLE THIS
(10 minutes)

Huddle up with your team just before you dismiss.

Ask This:

1. God doesn't want us thinking about negative things, scary things, bad things or things that make us worried. If you want to – share one thought that you have struggled with which left you sad, scared or nervous.

2. When do you struggle most with your thoughts? Is it bedtime? In the morning before school? When you're away from your family? What is one way you could **KICK THE HABIT** of thinking bad thoughts during those times?

3. What is the "W" plan? What are some true, lovely, pure, excellent, worthy of praise things that you can think about this week?

Repeat This: *"Fix your thoughts on what is true, and honorable, and right, and pure, and lovely, and admirable. Think about things that are excellent and worthy of praise."* –Philippians 4:8

Pray This: *"Dear Jesus, I want the Holy Spirit to control my thoughts. Help me kick the habit of thinking about things that aren't good, helpful, or pleasing to you. I want to honor you in the way I think. Amen."*

Doodle This: *Have the boys turn to the Doodle page in their workbook (or copy it for them).*

PARENT CONNECTION

Our minds are a battlefield! We've all experienced the struggle to keep our thoughts focused on the positive, and our sons are no different. Many of our kids are struggling with worry, anxiety, and fear, and this war is being waged in their minds!

The Bible gives us SO many tools to remind us that our thoughts don't have to be troubled. This week we talked about practicing self-control in the things we think about. We cautioned the boys that our minds are a really easy place to grow bad fruit, but the Holy Spirit has promised to help us control the things we think about. If we ask Him, He'll help us replace our bad thoughts with good thoughts.

We gave the boys three main points to help them keep their thoughts under control. First, we encouraged them to let the Holy Spirit be the boss of their brain. Romans 8:6 tells us that letting the Spirit control our minds will lead to life and peace. When we put the Holy Spirit in charge, He will help us keep our minds thinking the best and not the worst.

Second, we encouraged the boys to "Kick the Habit" of bad thinking. Many of us have become accustomed to thinking negatively about certain things. Or sometimes we have a certain time of day or activity when our thoughts seem to just get away from us. We challenged the boys to "catch themselves" thinking negative things and quickly change those negative thoughts to positive ones.

Last, we taught the boys the "W" plan, which comes from Philippians 4:8: *"Finally, brothers and sisters, whatever is true, whatever is noble, whatever is right, whatever is pure, whatever is lovely, whatever is admirable – if anything is excellent or praiseworthy – think about such things."* This is a great verse to help us analyze the content of our thought life. When you have a thought, filter it through the "W" list—Is it true? Is it lovely? Is it pure? If it's not, get it out of your brain!

One thing I know for sure is that God does not want His children to be anxious, worried, fearful, negative, or consumed by worst-case scenarios. Encourage your son to practice self-control in his thought life, and I believe His peace will come to his heart and mind.

Bazooka Boys ★ Who Am I?

Bazooka Boys ★ Who Am I?

 **TAKE HOME ACTIVITY**

WEEK 3

KINDERGARTEN AND 1ST GRADE

God wants you to think about good things! In the picture below, circle the GOOD things and put an X through the BAD things.

God wants us to think about good things! In the verse below, fill in the blank with the word that starts with the same letter!

Word List

True

Honorable

Right

Pure

Lovely

Admirable

Excellent

Worthy

"Fix your thoughts on what is T_____, and H_____, and R_____, and P_____, and L_____, and A_____. Think about things that are E_____ and W_____ of praise."

–Philippians 4:8

Now find the words here!

```
Y P W Z W Y C I P D Z X T M A
H U A V A A L Q T R W E N D G
T R M Q Y H Y E S R S B M F S
R E A V J O H O V I U I M T G
O H O W F N A A A O R E W G V
W V X Y W O Y R H A L A F H D
Y F I G F R P T B P A J D P A
Q V Z H O A Z L Z K J N W K Q
D B F M A B E C C U G E S Q D
S X B Y D L T N E L L E C X E
G G W G P E P F L S I V K R G
W Z Y T T J A C G L H Y B L D
Z M W E E H O X R I G H T V B
E M F P R X I N M E V I I A J
P V Q E L C W P B P J J Z G J
```

Word List

Admirable

Excellent

Honorable

Lovely

Praise

Pure

Right

True

Worthy

Bazooka Boys ★ Who Am I?

TAKE HOME ACTIVITY

WEEK 3

2ND AND 3RD GRADE

Look up Proverbs 4:23 in your Bible. Write it out here:

God wants us to be careful with the things we think about. Inside the picture, write some negative things you sometimes think about. Then cross them out and write positive things instead!

Bazooka Boys ★ Who Am I?

God wants us to think about good things! In the verse below, fill in the blank with the word that starts with the same letter!

Word List

Excellent

Worthy

Pure

Lovely

Honorable

True

Right

Admirable

"*Fix your thoughts on what is* T_____, *and* H_____, *and* R_____, *and* P_____, *and* L_____, *and* A_____. *Think about things that are* E_____ *and* W_____ *of praise.*"

–Philippians 4:8

Now find the words here!

```
Y P W Z W Y C I P D Z X T M A
H U A V A A L Q T R W E N D G
T R M Q Y H Y E S R S B M F S
R E A V J O H O V I U I M T G
O H O W F N A A A O R E W G V
W V X Y W O Y R H A L A F H D
Y F I G F R P T B P A J D P A
Q V Z H O A Z L Z K J N W K Q
D B F M A B E C C U G E S Q D
S X B Y D L T N E L L E C X E
G G W G P E P F L S I V K R G
W Z Y T T J A C G L H Y B L D
Z M W E E H O X R I G H T V B
E M F P R X I N M E V I I A J
P V Q E L C W P B P J J Z G J
```

Word List

Admirable

Excellent

Honorable

Lovely

Praise

Pure

Right

True

Worthy

Bazooka Boys ★ Who Am I?

4TH AND 5TH GRADE

Look up Proverbs 4:23 in your Bible. Write it out here:

God wants us to be careful with the things we think about. Inside the picture, write some negative things you sometimes think about. Then cross them out and write positive things instead!

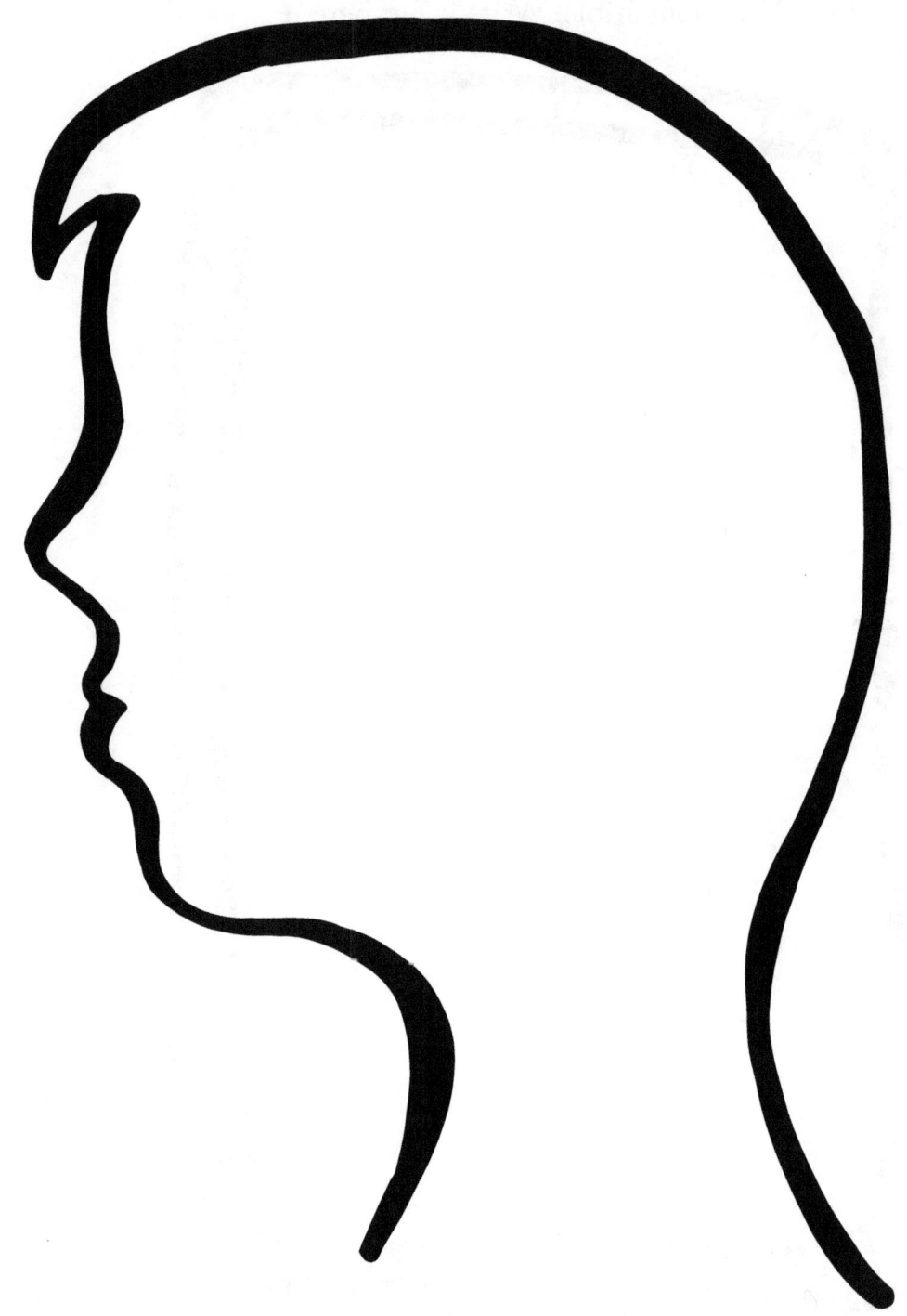

Bazooka Boys ★ Who Am I?

Philippians 4:8 gives us the formula for our "W" test! Look up the verse and fill in the blanks with all the good things we're supposed to think about.

1. _____
2. _____
3. _____
4. _____
5. _____
6. _____
7. _____
8. _____

Now find the words here!

```
Y P W Z W Y C I P D Z X T M A
H U A V A A L Q T R W E N D G
T R M Q Y H E S R S B M F S
R E A V J O H O V I U I M T G
O H O W F N A A A O R E W G V
W V X Y W O Y R H A L A F H D
Y F I G F R P T B P A J D P A
Q V Z H O A Z L Z K J N W K Q
D B F M A B E C C U G E S Q D
S X B Y D L T N E L L E C X E
G G W G P E P F L S I V K R G
W Z Y T T J A C G L H Y B L D
Z M W E E H O X R I G H T V B
E M F P R X I N M E V I I A J
P V Q E L C W P B P J J Z G J
```

Word List

Admirable

Excellent

Honorable

Lovely

Praise

Pure

Right

True

Worthy

Bazooka Boys ★ Who Am I?

WEEK 3

BAZOOKA BLAST OVERVIEW: WEEK 4

Large Group Lesson: *(15 minutes)*

- Our words are powerful. Once we say something, we cannot take it back.

- Clean words come from a clean heart. If your words aren't clean, you need to take a look at what is going on inside of you.

- Sometimes the best thing we can do it to just STOP talking.

- T.H.I.N.K. before you speak!

Bazooka Blitz: Small Group Time:

    Bible Blitz *(10 minutes)*

        Bible Verse Relay *(Instructions on page 91)*

    Bazooka Project *(20 minutes)*

        T.H.I.N.K. Launcher *(Instructions on page 93)*

    Team Huddle *(10 minutes)*

      <u>Ask This:</u>

      1. What did we learn from the lesson of the tube of toothpaste? Why is that so important to remember?
      2. Today we learned that clean words come from a clean heart. What could be going on inside someone's heart to make them say mean words?
      3. Do you remember what the T.H.I.N.K. principle is? Let's practice saying it together. Is it: True, Helpful, Inspiring, Necessary, Kind?

    <u>Repeat This:</u> *"Let the words of my mouth and the thoughts of my heart be pleasing to you O Lord."* —Psalm 19:14

    <u>Pray This:</u> *"Dear Jesus, I want to honor You with the words that I say. Please cleanse my heart and make it clean. And help me to choose my words carefully so that others will want to know more about you. Amen."*

    <u>Doodle This:</u> Copy the Doodle page (or have them turn to that page in their workbook)

WATCH YOUR MOUTH

What's the Point?
Our words have power, so we should be careful what we say.

THEME VERSE
"Let the words of my mouth and the thoughts of my heart be pleasing to you O Lord."
Psalm 19:14

RELATED BIBLE PASSAGE
James 1:26

★ LARGE GROUP LESSON ★
(15 minutes)

Joshua's little sister was **SUCH** a pain! She was always coming into his room and messing with his stuff. She spied on him and his friends and told everyone their private conversations. She drove him crazy, and the more angry he got, the more she seemed determined to annoy him.

His frustration was growing and growing, and he found himself saying really mean things back at her. He knew it wasn't right, but he couldn't seem to stop himself from screaming at her. He kept trying to justify his reaction by telling himself, "She deserves it!" or "If she would leave me alone, I wouldn't have to yell at her!"

But one day he was reading his Bible when he came across James 1:26: *"You might think you are a very religious person. But if your tongue is out of control, you are fooling yourself"* (ERV).

What does it mean for your **TONGUE** to be out of control? It means you aren't using self-control to make sure the words that come out of your mouth are kind to others and pleasing to God.

Joshua realized the words he was saying to his sister were not okay. Even though she was wrong, it didn't make his behavior any better. He knew that if he wanted to show God how much he loved Him, he would need to do a better job choosing the words he said to his sister.

The Bible tells us over and over again that our words matter. It's crazy how many verses in the Bible are about watching what you say! Why do you think God took the time to talk to us about this?

Bazooka Boys ★ Who Am I?

BECAUSE OUR WORDS ARE POWERFUL.

Raise your hand if you can remember something NICE or ENCOURAGING someone has said to you.

Now raise your hand if you can remember something MEAN or HURTFUL someone has said to you.

Think of how you feel when someone says something nice to you. It can change your whole day! It can make you want to try something new. You feel happy, encouraged, and strong when someone says something good.

Now, think of how you feel when someone says something mean or unkind. IT'S THE WORST! When someone says something hurtful, it can make you feel horrible. Those mean words can stick with you for a really, really long time and make you feel bad about yourself.

Why? Because our words are powerful.

That's why it's so important to be careful about what we say. It can be so easy to have a thought and then let it slip out of your mouth without ever thinking about what those words might do to another person, but the truth is that our words are a big, big deal. Proverbs 13:3 says, *"Those who control their tongue will have a long life; opening your mouth can ruin everything."*

OBJECT LESSON: Toothpaste tube

Supplies:
- One tube of toothpaste
- Bowl or plate
- Paper towels for cleanup

(Have a volunteer come to the front and ask him to squeeze the toothpaste out of the tube onto the plate. Once he has squeezed out a bunch of the toothpaste, ask him to put the toothpaste back into the tube.)

"Once the toothpaste comes out of the tube, you cannot put it back in. It's the same with our words—once they come out, you can't put them back in again. You can apologize and try and make it right, but once the words come out of your mouth, they go right into the hearts of your family members and friends, and you cannot take them back."

Our words have the power to hurt others, and once you say them, you can't take them back. Even if you're really sorry and apologize, the words you said have already done their damage. This is why it's important to learn to control your tongue and **STOP** yourself from saying things you shouldn't say.

OBJECT LESSON: Broken pencil

(Hold up a pencil and break it in two.)

"When we say words that hurt others, we do damage. We hurt people's feelings, we make others feel bad, and we can disrespect our parents or teachers.

Now, I can say sorry to the pencil. But is it still broken?

I can take tape and try and fix it. I can try and glue it together. But it is still broken.

You and I can do damage to our friends and family if we don't use self-control. Even though we all make mistakes, and God can help us fix it when we hurt our friends, it's much, much easier to choose our words carefully than to try and fix the damage after we say the wrong thing."

So how can we choose good words?

 **1. CLEAN WORDS COME FROM A CLEAN HEART.**

Luke 6:45 says, "*A good man says good things. These come from the good that is stored up in his heart. An evil man says evil things. These come from the evil that is stored up in his heart. A person's mouth says everything that is in their heart.*" If the words coming out of your mouth are not good words, then you need to look at what's going on in your heart.

OBJECT LESSON:

(Take a paper grocery sack, and draw a face on it. Cut out the portion where the mouth should be. Fill the bag with slips of paper that say mean or unkind things.)

Examples:
- You're stupid.
- I hate you.
- You're ugly.
- I hate what you made for dinner!
- No one likes you!
- I DON'T WAAAAANT TO!
- Did you hear the news about Sally? We shouldn't play with her cause she's so weird.

(Have the kids take turns putting their hands inside the mouth and pulling out a piece of paper and reading what it says.)

"Where are these horrible things coming from? They're coming from what's going on inside! The same is true with us. The things coming out of our mouths are coming from what's inside our hearts."

If you find yourself saying mean, unkind, or inappropriate words, you need to take a good look at your heart. Are you angry inside? Are you scared about something and lashing out at others? Are you feeling bad about yourself, so it seems okay to hurt others, too? Or maybe you've just gotten careless about choosing the right words and you just let your first thought come out instead of practicing self-control?

If you're having a problem with your words, the first thing to do is to look at your heart. Ask Jesus to take away the bad things in your heart that seem to be coming out of your mouth. Pray the prayer King David prayed in Psalm 51:10: "*Create in me a clean heart, O God.*" A clean heart is the first step to having clean words.

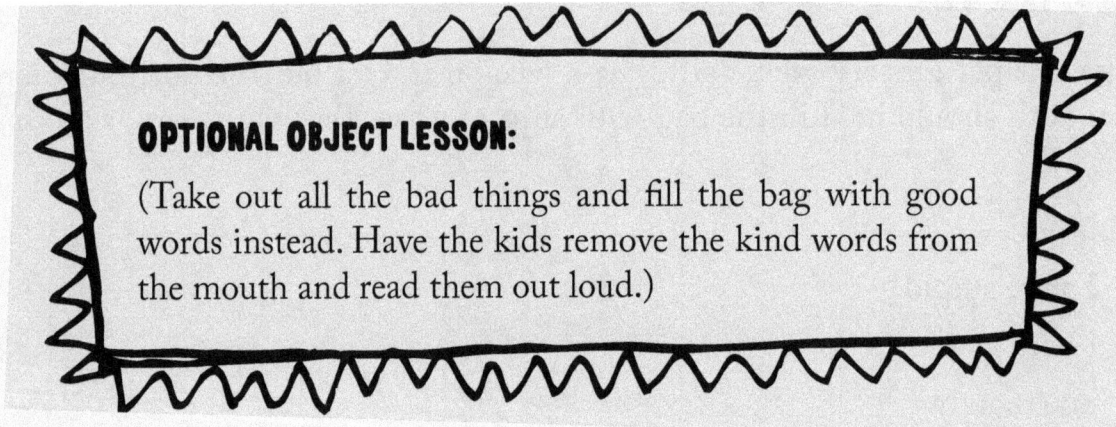

OPTIONAL OBJECT LESSON:
(Take out all the bad things and fill the bag with good words instead. Have the kids remove the kind words from the mouth and read them out loud.)

Examples:
- You did such a great job!
- I'm sorry.
- I'm frustrated. Can we talk through our problem?
- Can I help?
- I'm so glad you're my friend!
- I'm sorry, but I don't talk about my friends when they aren't here.

REMEMBER THAT CLEAN WORDS COME FROM A CLEAN HEART.

The second way we can choose good words is to...

 **2. STOP TALKING!**

So often, we find ourselves saying things we shouldn't. Many times we KNOW we shouldn't share that secret or yell at our friend or repeat that word you know is inappropriate, but sometimes we just don't make the right choice in the moment. One of the best ways to help control yourself is simply by saying **"STOP!"**

When you feel yourself starting to say something mean, close your mouth and imagine putting a piece of tape over it. When you start to repeat that juicy piece of gossip about a friend, close your mouth and pretend to lock your lips together and throw away the key. When you're tempted to whine when your mom asks you to set the dinner table, press your lips together **AS TIGHT AS YOU CAN** and repeat inside to yourself, "I will not whine! I will not whine!"

Sometimes the very best thing you can do to control your tongue is just stop talking. There's a verse in the Bible that says, *"A person who talks too much gets into trouble. A wise person learns to be quiet"* (Proverbs 10:19, ERV). A really good way to practice self-control with your words is to simply stop talking when you don't have anything nice to say.

So, clean words come from a clean heart, STOP talking, and lastly…

 ## 3. t.H.I.N.K. BEFORE YOU SPEAK!

So often, we say whatever pops into our heads. We don't stop to think about the words and how they'll affect the people around us. I learned a really great way to check out my words **BEFORE** I say them. Here's how it works—before you speak, ask yourself, "Is this…"

TRUE?

HELPFUL?

INSPIRING?

NECESSARY?

KIND?

Silas heard the craziest news about his friend Seth—he had failed a math test and his mom was going to have to come into school to talk to the teacher. At recess, a bunch of the boys came over and began asking him questions about Seth. They were sharing all kinds of rumors and gossip about the situation. Some people were saying he cheated, others were saying he was going to be grounded, and others were just laughing.

Silas stopped for a moment and decided to **t.H.I.N.K** before he spoke. First of all, many of the things the guys said were **NOT TRUE**. Secondly, nothing the boys said was **HELPFUL**. It wasn't helping Seth at all to have his friends talking about him when he wasn't there to defend himself. It also wasn't **INSPIRING**. This conversation wasn't focusing on good things, it was focusing on bad things. Silas also wondered if it was **NECESSARY** to talk through the issues with these boys. It didn't seem right to talk about what had happened without Seth being there. And lastly, he asked himself if it was **KIND** to talk to his other friends about something that might be embarrassing to Seth. He realized he would be hurt if the same thing happened to him, so he decided the conversation wasn't **KIND**.

Once Silas went through his **t.H.I.N.K** list, he was convinced he shouldn't be having that conversation. He told the other guys that he didn't think it was cool to talk about this and he turned around and walked away. Although it could have been really easy to just go along with his friends, Silas decided to **t.H.I.N.K.** before he spoke.

Our words are powerful. The things we say can build people up or tear them down. They can make people feel better or make them feel worse. They can honor our parents and teachers, or they can show disrespect. They can be honest, or they can be full of lies. They can be grateful, or they can be whining and complaining.

Colossians 4:6 says, *"Let your conversations always be full of grace and seasoned with salt."* When something is seasoned with salt, it makes people thirsty! When our conversations are filled with grace (kind and good things), people will be thirsty to know more about Jesus. There's nothing I want more than that! So let's choose our words carefully and practice self-control.

Bazooka Boys ★ Who Am I?

BIBLE VERSE RELAY

(10 minutes)

Supplies

- Notecards

Prep

- Write the verse and reference on the notecards, one word per card. You should end up with 20 cards. (*"Let the words of my mouth and the thoughts of my heart be pleasing to you O Lord."* Psalm 19:14)
- Draw a starting line at one end of the room and a finish line at the other end of the room. (Tape works well for this!)

Directions

1. Divide the boys into teams and give each boy one card each. Make sure the words are not in order! (You may have to have some boys go twice)

2. Have the boys line up behind the starting line. When you say "Go," the first boy in line runs to the finish line and places his card down. He should then run back and tag the next boy in line. Each boy adds his word and tries to place his card in the correct order. Once the entire verse is at the finish line, the whole team should run to the finish line and yell the verse out as loud as they can!

3. The first team to recite the verse wins!

Bazooka Boys ★ Who Am I?

BAZOOKA PROJECT

THINK LAUNCHER

(20 minutes)

Supplies

- 3 cardboard tubes (Paper towel sized)
- Wooden Spoon
- 4 rubber bands
- Pom Poms, marshmallows, scrunched up balls of paper or other soft items for launching
- 5 cups labeled with a letter (T. H. I. N. K.)
- *You may want to make 2 or 3 launchers depending on how many boys you have in your group.

Directions

1. Lay two of the cardboard tubes side by side and then place the third tube on top to form a triangle shaped stack.

2. Fasten the tubes together with a rubber band on each end.

3. Next, position the wooden spoon at the front of the tubes, and loop a rubber band over the top of the spoon, stretch it around the tubes and then bring it back over itself at the top of the spoon so it holds the spoon to the tubes.

4. Finally, take the last rubber band, loop it over the handle of the wooden spoon, take it around the cardboard tubes, and back over the spoon.

5. Have the boys take turns launching the pompoms at the cups. If a pompom lands in a cup, they boy must yell out what that letter means! (True, Helpful, Inspiring, Necessary, Kind)

Bazooka Boys ★ Who Am I?

ASK THIS ★ REPEAT THIS ★ PRAY THIS ★ DOODLE THIS
(10 minutes)

Huddle up with your team just before you dismiss.

Ask This:

1. What did we learn from the lesson of the tube of toothpaste? Why is that so important to remember?

2. Today we learned that clean words come from a clean heart. What could be going on inside someone's heart to make them say mean words?

3. Do you remember what the T.H.I.N.K. principle is? Let's practice saying it together. Is it:

>   TRUE
>   HELPFUL
>   INSPIRING
>   NECESSARY
>   KIND

Repeat This:

Let the words of my mouth and the thoughts of my heart be pleasing to you O Lord."
—Psalm 19:14

Pray This:

"Dear Jesus, I want to honor You with the words that I say. Please cleanse my heart and make it clean. And help me to choose my words carefully so that others will want to know more about you. Amen."

Doodle This:

Copy the Doodle page for the boys *(or have them turn to that page in their workbook)*.

PARENT CONNECTION

We've all heard the saying, "Sticks and stones can break my bones, but words will never hurt me." And we all know how painfully false that statement is! This week we taught the boys that our words are powerful. They have the power to encourage someone and they also have the power to tear someone down and harm them. We showed the boys a tube of toothpaste—once you squeeze all the toothpaste out, you can't put it back inside the tube. Like the toothpaste, once words come out of our mouths, we can't take them back. We need to use self-control **BEFORE** we speak our words out loud.

Luke 6:45 says, *"A good man says good things. These come from the good that is stored up in his heart. And evil man says evil things. These come from the evil that is stored up in his heart. A person's mouth says everything that is in their heart."* We reminded the boys that clean words come from a clean heart. If we find ourselves constantly tearing others down, using inappropriate words, or sharing things we should not share, our first job is to look at our hearts and ask God to help us have a clean heart.

Second, we told them that sometimes the very best thing we can do is JUST **STOP TALKING!** We encouraged them to put their hands over their mouths to keep themselves from blurting out things they will regret later if necessary (a lesson we all could use from time to time)!

Last, we taught the boys the acronym **T.H.I.N.K.** Before you share something, ask yourself the following questions:

1. Is it True?
2. Is it Helpful?
3. Is it Inspiring?
4. Is it Necessary?
5. Is it Kind?

If you can't answer "yes" to all these questions, perhaps you should keep quiet. Controlling the tongue is not an easy task, but God has promised to help us if we will do our part by watching the words we use and being careful to only speak life!

Bazooka Boys ★ Who Am I?

DOODLE PAGE

LESSON 4

Clean words come from a clean heart, in the word bubbles next to the dark heart, write some words that can come from a heart that is not clean. In the word bubbles next to the white heart, write some words that can come from a clean heart.

Bazooka Boys ★ Who Am I?

TAKE HOME ACTIVITY

KINDERGARTEN AND 1ST GRADE

Ephesians 4:29 says, "*When you talk, don't say anything bad. But say the good things that people need—whatever will help them grow stronger. Then what you say will be a blessing to those who hear you*" (ERV). Our superheroes are encouraging one another! Write the following words in the bubbles and then color the picture! Good words:

    Way to go!   Nice job!

    You're amazing!   You're super strong!

Bazooka Boys ★ Who Am I?

TAKE HOME ACTIVITY

2ND AND 3RD GRADE

Ephesians 4:29 says, *"When you talk, don't say anything bad. But say the good things that people need—whatever will help them grow stronger. Then what you say will be a blessing to those who hear you"* (ERV). Our superheroes are encouraging one another! Write the following words in the bubbles and then color the picture! Good words:

Way to go!	Nice job!
You're amazing!	You're super strong!

Look up Proverbs 12:18 in your Bible and write it out below:

Bazooka Boys ★ Who Am I?

Use the key to solve the word problem below.

Ephesians 4:29

A	B	D	E	G	H	I	K	L	M	N	O	P	R	S	T	U	V	W	Y
15	5	23	8	16	19	7	6	14	17	10	11	3	1	26	20	4	21	13	24

"When you talk, don't
say anything bad.
But say the good
things that people
need — whatever will
help them grow
stronger. Then what
you say will be a
blessing to those
who hear you."

Bazooka Boys ★ Who Am I?

TAKE HOME ACTIVITY

4TH AND 5TH GRADE

Look up the following verses in your Bible and write them below:

Psalm 141:3   Proverbs 18:21   Proverbs 12:14   Proverbs 12: 18

WEEK 4

Use the key to solve the word problem below.

Ephesians 4:29

A	B	D	E	G	H	I	K	L	M	N	O	P	R	S	T	U	V	W	Y
15	5	23	8	16	19	7	6	14	17	10	11	3	1	26	20	4	21	13	24

"W H E N   Y O U   T A L K ,   D O N ' T
13 19 8 10   24 11 4   20 15 14 6   23 11 10   20

S A Y   A N Y T H I N G   B A D.
26 15 24   15 10 24 20 19 7 10 16   5 15 23

B U T   S A Y   T H E   G O O D
5 4 20   26 15 24   20 19 8   16 11 11 23

T H I N G S   T H A T   P E O P L E
20 19 7 10 16 26   20 19 15 20   3 8 11 3 14 8

N E E D — W H A T E V E R   W I L L
10 8 8 23   13 19 15 20 8 21 8 1   13 7 14 14

H E L P   T H E M   G R O W
19 8 14 3   20 19 8 17   16 1 11 13

S T R O N G E R.   T H E N   W H A T
26 20 1 11 10 16 8 1   20 19 8 10   13 19 15 20

Y O U   S A Y   W I L L   B E   A
24 11 4   26 15 24   13 7 14 14   5 8   15

B L E S S I N G   T O   T H O S E
5 14 8 26 26 7 10 16   20 11   20 19 11 26 8

W H O   H E A R   Y O U."
13 19 11   19 8 15 1   24 11 4

Bazooka Boys ★ Who Am I?

WEEK 4

BAZOOKA BLAST OVERVIEW: WEEK 5

Large Group Lesson: *(15 minutes)*

- Everything we have has been given to us by God!
- We need to give back to God what belongs to Him by giving a tithe.
- We need to take good care of the things God has given us.
- God wants us to be generous with our things!

Bazooka Blitz: Small Group Time:

    Bible Blitz *(10 minutes)*
        Penny Relay *(Instructions on page 117)*
    Bazooka Project *(20 minutes)*
        Duct Tape Wallet *(Instructions on page 118)*
    Team Huddle *(10 minutes)*

      <u>Ask This:</u>

1. One of the biggest ways we can practice self-control with our money is by giving back to God what belongs to Him! Who remember what a tithe is? Where do we give our tithe and what does God do with it?
2. Another way we can practice self-control with our money is by taking care of the stuff God gives us. What are some ways we can take care of the things God has given us? (*Destructiveness, Wastefulness, Irresponsibility*)
3. What should we do before we spend money? (*Stop and think before you spend!*) What three things did we learn today to help us take care of the money God gives us? Share – Save – Spend!

<u>Repeat This:</u> *"And God will generously provide all you need. Then you will always have everything you need and plenty left over to share with others."* – 2 Corinthians 9:8

<u>Pray This:</u> *"Dear God, Thank you for always providing everything I need. Help me to take good care of the things you have given me, and to be generous with others! Amen."*

<u>Doodle This:</u> Have the boys turn to the Doodle page in their workbook (or copy it for them).

Bazooka Boys ★ Who Am I?

MONEY MATTERS

WHAT'S THE POINT?

Everything we have comes from God, and we need to do whatever Jesus tells us to do with our money and things

THEME VERSE

And God will generously provide all you need. Then you will always have everything you need and plenty left over to share with others.
2 Corinthians 9:8

RELATED BIBLE PASSAGE

John 6:5–15

★ LARGE GROUP LESSON ★
(15 minutes)

Has anyone ever given you money? Maybe you got a five-dollar bill in a birthday card from your grandparents? Or maybe your parents gave you a dollar for doing an extra chore? Or maybe you found a quarter on the ground?

Do you want to hear something really cool? The Bible tells us **GOD** is the one who gives us money. I know that can seem crazy because it seems like our money is given to us by other people. But the truth is, when someone gives you money, they're doing it because God wants them to do it. God is in charge of ALL the money in the whole world, and He gives it to us to use for the things He wants us to use it for.

First Chronicles 29:14 says, *"Everything comes from you. We've given back to you only what comes from you."* And verse 16 of that same chapter says, *"But all of it comes from you. All of it belongs to you"* (NIRV).

God owns all the money in the entire universe, and He gives it to us to use. Another cool verse—Psalm 50:12—says, *"I already own the world and everything in it"* (ERV). Everything in the whole world belongs to God. He's the boss.

One cool thing about God is that He gives us money to buy things. He gives your parents jobs so they can earn money to pay for your house and food. He gives your grandparents money so they can come visit you. He gives **YOU** money to buy toys, treats, and lots of other things.

It's so important to remember that everything we have belongs to God. That means our money and all our things! When we remember that, it changes the way we take care of what we have.

Bazooka Boys ★ Who Am I?

ILLUSTRATION:

(Have 10 treats with you—suckers, pieces of gum, etc. Invite someone to the front, and tell them you would like them to help you with your treats. Keep reminding them that they are **YOURS**. You own them and they belong to you, **BUT** you are giving them to hold onto and use for certain things. You are asking them to be your helper! Keep this illustration going throughout the large group lesson.)

So what does it mean to have self-control with our money and the other things God has given us to take care of? Practicing self-control means we don't do things without thinking—and we make sure we do the things God wants us to do! When it comes to our money, we need to make sure we think about the way God wants us to use the things he's given us to hold.

What are some ways we can have self-control with our money and things?

1. GIVE BACK TO GOD WHAT HE ASKS YOU TO GIVE.

Andrew saw his mom with a calculator, her computer, and a checkbook. He asked his mom what she was doing, and she said, "I'm paying bills." Andrew was curious, so he asked, "What's the very first bill you pay?" Andrew's mom replied, "Oh, that's easy. The very first check I write is to our church! I know God has provided money for our family, so I make sure I give my very first offering to Him!"

Have you ever heard the word "tithe"? It's a funny word that comes up several times in the Bible. The first place it's mentioned is in Deuteronomy 14:22–23, which says, *"You must set aside a tithe of your crops—one-tenth of all the crops you harvest each year. Bring this tithe to the designated place of worship..."* People would bring the **VERY** best of their crops and animals to the Temple and give them back to God. They brought ten percent of everything they grew as an offering to God!

ILLUSTRATION:

(Refer back to the volunteer with the treat.)

"Tithing means we give ten percent back to God. So using my friend here as an example—since you have 10 items, you would give one back to me!"

(Have the student give you one treat back as a "tithe.")

When we tithe, we're reminding ourselves that all our money REALLY belongs to God. It's a way of saying "THANK YOU" for all the things He's provided for us!

Now what that means is that whatever money you and I get, we give ten percent back to God's work. Most people give their tithes to the church they go to. Churches use that money to help tell other people about Jesus. So when you tithe, you're helping the people in your community hear how much Jesus loves them. That's a pretty awesome way to spend your money!

The second way you can practice self-control with your money is to…

 ## 2. TAKE CARE OF THE STUFF GOD GIVES YOU!

ILLUSTRATION:

(Refer to the volunteer with the treat.)

"What would happen if my friend here didn't take good care of my things?"
"What if he started stomping on them and destroyed them?"

(Have the student stomp on the item or tear it apart.)

"What if he opened one up, started licking it, and then decided he didn't like that flavor and just threw it away?"

(Have the student do this as well.)

"What if he kept losing the suckers I asked him to hold for me? Not a one-time accident, but over and over again, not taking responsibility. Would he be a good helper to me?"

(Have the student throw three or four of the items over his shoulder so it's "lost.")

God has given you and me so many things, and one way we can show Him our appreciation is by taking good care of the stuff He gives us. That means not destroying things. That means not being wasteful with food, or toys, or lots of other stuff. It also means being responsible for the things God has put us in charge of. When we show respect for the things God has given us, it's another way of saying "Thank You!" to God for being so generous with us!

And the last way we can practice self-control with our money is to...

 ## 3. BE GENEROUS.

God gives us money so we can pay our bills, have food to eat, and have clothes to wear. But He also gives us money so we can use it to help other people. We need to always ask Jesus if there's anything special He wants us to do with His money.

There's a story in the Bible about a little boy who was determined to share what he had with Jesus to help other people. Jesus was teaching lots of people—around 4,000 of them! They had been sitting there for a long time, and they were all starting to get really, really hungry! There were no restaurants in those days (So sad—no McDonalds!). Everyone was wondering what to do when a little boy came to Jesus and said, "I will share my lunch!" So Jesus took the boy's lunch, which had five loaves of bread and two fish in it, and prayed over it. Then the coolest miracle happened—God multiplied the food, and there was enough to feed every single person with baskets of food left over!

SHARE. SAVE. SPEND.

What I love about this story is that the little boy was willing to share what He had to help others. God has given you lots and lots of things, and He wants you to use those things to help others. So be generous, and always ask Jesus if He wants you to share something you have with someone else. Matthew 10:42 says, *"And if you give even a cup of cold water to one of the least of my followers, you will surely be rewarded."* God might ask you to give someone food, it might be money, it might even be something as simple as a cup of water. But whatever Jesus asks you to do, just do it!

One really important thing to remember when we talk about having self-control with our money is that we need to be really careful how we use the things God has given us.

ILLUSTRATION:

(Refer back to the volunteer with the treat.)

"Now, I gave you 10 items when we started. How many do you have left? Well, you gave one back to me as a tithe. But then you wasted a couple and lost a couple, too."

"Well, the next thing I was going to ask you to do was to give a treat to the rest of the kids in class. Do you have enough to do that? Why not? Because you already used them for other things!"

(If you want, you can have an extra set of treats to hand out as an illustration of what it means to be generous. Give one to each child!)

It's so fun to have money to spend! As soon as that money finds its way into your pocket, you start imagining all the things you can buy with your cash. Maybe you love to buy gum or candy. Maybe you want to save up for a special toy. Or maybe you want to spend your money on a gift for someone you care about.

But **BEFORE** you do that, God wants you to **STOP**, **THINK**, and **ASK** Him how He wants you to handle your money. Too often we just go and spend all our money without thinking. Many of us run out and spend our money and then think about it later. But a really good rule to remember is to **THINK** first, and spend second. Think, "Is this what God wants me to do with my money? Does He want me to be generous to someone first? Should I save this money to buy something bigger later? Are my parents okay with me spending my money this way?"

Don't just spend without thinking! Think first, and then spend!

God wants us to do three things with our money: Share. Save. Spend. Share what you have with God and others. Then save some money for things you may need later. And then spend and enjoy what God has provided for you!

Bazooka Boys ★ Who Am I?

WEEK 5

PENNY RELAY
(10 minutes)

Supplies
- Pennies (10 per boy)
- Plastic cups (3 per team)
- Sharpie
- Plastic spoons (1 per boy)
- Tape
- Table

Prep
- Create a starting line using a piece of tape or some other marker.
- At the other end of the room, place a cup on a table across from each team.
- Label one cup TITHE and place it in somewhere else in the room.

Directions
1. Divide the boys into two teams.
2. Hand each boy a spoon and 10 pennies.
3. Have them line up at the starting line.
4. When it's their turn, have them place the spoon in their mouth, and place 5 pennies on the spoon and run to the other side of the room and drop the pennies in the cup.
5. They then run back and tag the next player in line.
6. Each player should run 2 rounds, so they drop a total of 10 pennies in the cup.
7. On the third round, the players run to the table, remove 1 of the pennies and drop it in the TITHE cup.
8. First team to "pay their tithe" wins!
9. Make sure you explain what a tithe is, and remind the boys that we give back to God what belongs to Him!

Bazooka Boys ★ Who Am I?

DUCT TAPE WALLETS

(20 minutes)

Supplies

- Plain or patterned Duct tape (approx. 10 ft. per boy)
- Scissors
- Ruler

*Note: Younger boys will need help with this. Consider precutting strips for them or creating the pieces ahead of time.

Directions

1. Cut four 10 inch strips of duct tape and create a wide sheet by overlapping the edges.
2. Repeat step one and then place the two sticky sides of the sheets together to create the main part of your wallet.
3. Next, cut two 3 inch pieces of duct tape and place them sticky sides together to create your pocket. If desired, cut a contrasting piece of tape and fold over the top to make a fun edge.
4. Repeat step three so you have two pocket pieces.
5. Fold over your large sheet to create a long, skinny rectangle.
6. Place the 3 inch piece on the front left side of the wallet. Place the second 3 inch piece on the front right side of the wallet. Cut a 11 or 12 inch strip and place along the bottom of the wallet, half of the strip on the front and half on the back. Fold up the strip to secure the pockets in place. Trim the edges if necessary.
7. Cut a 7 inch piece of duct tape and place on the side of the wallet – half on the front and half on the back. Secure and trim as necessary. Repeat on the other side.

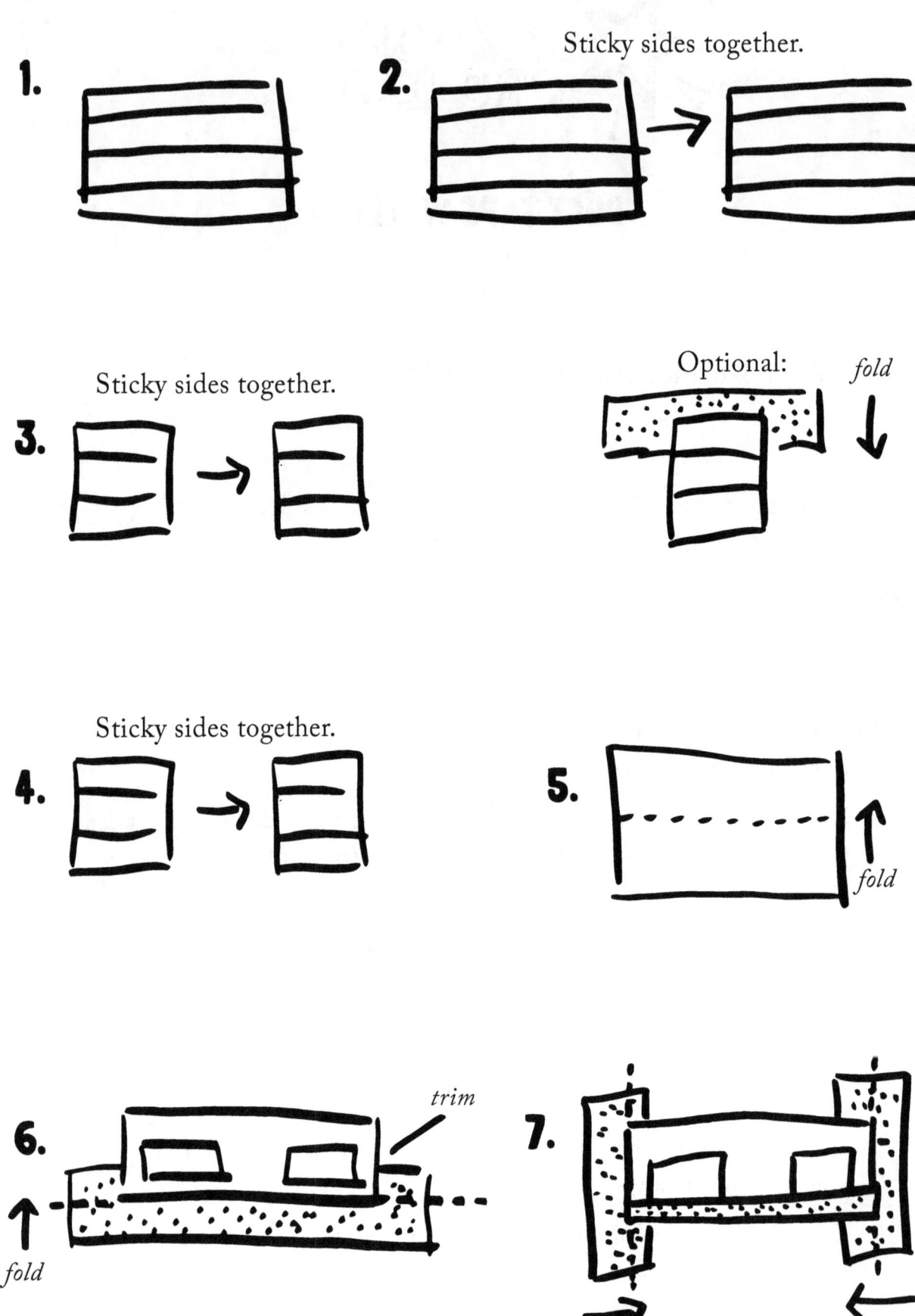

WEEK 5

ASK THIS ★ REPEAT THIS ★ PRAY THIS ★ DOODLE THIS
(10 minutes)

Huddle up with your team just before you dismiss.

Ask This:

1. One of the biggest ways we can practice self-control with our money is by giving back to God what belongs to Him! Who remember what a tithe is? Where do we give our tithe and what does God do with it?

2. Another way we can practice self-control with our money is by taking care of the stuff God gives us. What are some ways we can take care of the things God has given us? (*Destructiveness, Wastefulness, Irresponsibility*)

3. What should we do before we spend money? (*Stop and thing before you spend!*) What three things did we learn today to help us take care of the money God gives us? Share – Save – Spend!

Repeat This:

"And God will generously provide all you need. Then you will always have everything you need and plenty left over to share with others."
– 2 Corinthians 9:8

Pray This:

"Dear God, Thank you for always providing everything I need. Help me to take good care of the things you have given me, and to be generous with others! Amen."

Doodle This:
Have the boys turn to the Doodle page in their workbook (or copy it for them).

PARENT CONNECTION

Did you know there are more verses in the Bible about money than there are about love? Clearly, God wants us to train up our kids in many areas of life, including handling the resources He gives us! This is one of those areas where your **EXAMPLE** will speak louder than any lesson you could ever teach. It's important to demonstrate with your family resources what it means to live generously. Be consistent in giving, and tell your kids what you're doing. This is a lifelong lesson that will radically affect their lives.

We taught the boys today that everything we have comes from God. He generously gives us resources to use for His purposes. It's important to remember that all our money is God's…we just get to hold onto it for Him!

We shared about tithing and giving God ten percent of all the money we make. I strongly encourage you to start this practice early in your kids' lives. It's an important spiritual discipline that gets harder to implement the older you get!

We also talked about taking good care of the things God gives us. This includes being responsible for our things, not being destructive with our property, and not being wasteful. When we know everything we have belongs to God, there should be a level of respect for the things He has provided for us.

And finally we talked to the boys about generosity. God blesses us so we can bless others. We encouraged the boys to **THINK** before they **SPEND**, asking God if there's some way He would like them to be generous with their money or things. Many times we make impulsive decisions with our money, and then we don't have the resources left to be generous toward others.

God loves to bless His children. Learning the principles of honoring God with our money is important for all of us!

DOODLE PAGE

LESSON 5

A good way to take care of the money God gives us is to share, spend, and save! On the list below draw a picture of something you could share! Draw a picture of something you could save up for! And then draw a picture of something you want to spend your money on after you've been generous!

SHARE

SPEND

SAVE

Bazooka Boys ★ Who Am I?

KINDERGARTEN AND 1ST GRADE

John 6:1–15 tells the story of the little boy who shared his lunch with Jesus. Jesus took the fish and bread the boy gave Him and multiplied it to feed thousands of people! On the fish below, draw a picture or write out some things you have that you could share with others.

Our theme verse this week is 2 Corinthians 9:8. In the sentence below, write the word **NEED** in the blank spaces, then practice reading the verse out loud.

"And God will generously provide all you _____. Then you will always have everything you _____ and plenty left over to share with others" (2 Corinthians 9:8).

2ND AND 3RD GRADE

Our theme verse this week is 2 Corinthians 9:8. In the sentence below, write the word **NEED** in two of the blanks, and the word **SHARE** in the other blank, then practice reading the verse out loud.

"And God will generously provide all you _____. Then you will always have everything you _____ and plenty left over to _____ with others" (2 Corinthians 9:8).

Use the words about money and generosity below to complete the crossword puzzle.

Across
2. share
6. spend
7. generous
8. resources
9. save
10. money

Down
1. provide
3. responsible
4. belongs
5. tithe
7. give

Bazooka Boys ★ Who Am I?

TAKE HOME ACTIVITY

4TH AND 5TH GRADE

Look up 2 Corinthians 9:8 and write it out below. What do you think this verse means?

Use the words about money and generosity below to complete the crossword puzzle.

Across
2. share
6. spend
7. generous
8. resources
9. save
10. money

Down
1. provide
3. responsible
4. belongs
5. tithe
7. give

Bazooka Boys ★ Who Am I?

WEEK 5

Large Group Lesson: *(15 minutes)*

- We have all been given gifts by God and He wants us to use them!
- Take the time to figure out what your gifts are!
- We need to work hard at our gifts… that means practice, practice, practice!
- God wants us to share our gifts with others!.

Bazooka Blitz: Small Group Time:

Bible Blitz *(10 minutes)*

Practice Makes Perfect Basketball Shoot *(Instructions on page 143)*

Bazooka Project *(20 minutes)*

God's Gift Bingo *(Instructions on page 145)*

Team Huddle *(10 minutes)*

Ask This:

1. Where do our gifts come from? Does everyone have one?
2. Share one thing you're good at. Maybe it's a talent, a sport, a hobby, something at school, or even something about your personality that's unique and brings you or others joy.
3. What are some ways we can grow in our gifts? (*Possible Answers: Practice every day. Study—learn more. Ask people who are good at your talent to show you how to get better. Keep looking for opportunities to learn more about your talents.*)

Repeat This: "*God has given each of you a gift from his great variety of spiritual gifts. Use them well to serve one another.*" —1 Peter 4:10

Pray This: "*Dear God, Thank you for giving me gifts. I want to use them to the best of my ability. Help me work hard and get better. I want to use my gifts to show others how good you are. Amen.*"

Doodle This: Have the boys turn to the Doodle page in their workbook (or copy it for them).

Bazooka Boys ★ Who Am I?

USING MY GIFTS

What's the Point?
God has given each of us things we're good at, and we need to make sure we're doing everything we can to use our gifts!

THEME VERSE
God has given each of you a gift from his great variety of spiritual gifts.
1 Peter 4:10

RELATED BIBLE PASSAGE
Matthew 25:14–30

★ LARGE GROUP LESSON ★
(15 minutes)

Is there something you're REALLY good at doing? Maybe it's playing an instrument or doing science experiments? Maybe you love to read books or bake cakes? Maybe you love to fix things or play soccer?

Every single one of us has things we're good at—EVERY SINGLE ONE OF US. You know how I know that? Because the Bible tells us God has given each of us a gift or a talent. First Peter 4:10 says, *"God has given each of you a gift from his great variety of spiritual gifts. Use them well to serve one another."* That means when God created you, He made you good at certain things. Your gifts are probably different from my gifts, but you can be sure that God has put gifts inside of YOU!

Wasn't that so nice of God? I think it's pretty cool that He chose to give us things that would bring us so much joy! Our world could have just been filled with boring things that we all felt kind of excited about. Instead, He gave us things that we love, love, love to do!

And because we know our gifts were GIVEN to us by God, we can know God wants us to use our gifts the VERY best way we can. He wants us to work hard and practice and use them as much as possible. So when we talk about having self-control in every area of our lives, we should ask ourselves: Am I being self-controlled in the way I use my gifts?

God gave us talents, and He wants us to USE them. Imagine you pick out a gift for your mom for her birthday. You spend hours thinking about what you're going to get her. Then you spend hours shopping for just the right color and shape. And then you even go above the amount you were planning to spend just because you want to make her day extra special. You give it to her and you're so excited to give her such a special present.

Bazooka Boys ★ Who Am I?

A month later, you see the gift just sitting in the corner, still in the box, gathering dust. I can imagine you'd be pretty frustrated. You might think, "Hey, I spent a lot of time and energy on that gift, and you're doing **NOTHING** with it." I don't think you'd be very happy.

Some of you aren't taking very good care of the gifts God has given you. They're sitting on a shelf, gathering dust. You're not using the gifts and talents God has placed inside of you. I bet it makes God pretty sad to see gifts He's given us just sitting on the shelf, not being used or taken care of.

There's actually a story in the Bible where Jesus shares how He feels when people neglect the gifts and responsibilities He has given them.

ILLUSTRATION: Parable of the Talents Matthew 25:14–30, NIRV).

(Have four volunteers come up to the front. One will be the master, and three will be the servants. Have five bags of pennies for the first volunteer, two bags for the second volunteer, and one bag for the third volunteer. Read the story aloud and have the kids act it out.)

"At that time God's kingdom will also be like a man leaving home to travel to another place for a visit. Before he left, he talked with his servants. He told his servants to take care of his things while he was gone. He decided how much each servant would be able to care for. The man gave one servant five bags of money. He gave another servant two bags. And he gave a third servant one bag. Then he left. The servant who got five bags went quickly to invest the money. Those five bags of money earned five more. It was the same with the servant who had two bags. That servant invested the money and earned two more. But the servant who got one bag of money went away and dug a hole in the ground. Then he hid his master's money in the hole.

After a long time the master came home. He asked the servants what they did with his money. The servant who got five bags brought that amount and five more bags of money to the master. The servant said, 'Master, you trusted me to care for five bags of money. So I used them to earn five more.' The master answered, 'You did right. You are a good servant who can be trusted. You did well with that small amount of money. So I will let you care for much greater things. Come and share my happiness with me.' Then the servant who got two bags of money came to the master. The servant said, 'Master, you gave me two bags of money to care for. So I used your two bags to earn two more.' The master answered, 'You did right. You are a good servant who can be trusted. You did well with a small amount of money. So I will let you care for much greater things. Come and share my happiness with me.' Then the servant who got one bag of money came to the master. The servant said, 'Master, I knew you were a very hard man. You harvest what you did not plant. You gather crops where you did not put any seed. So I was afraid. I went and hid your money in the ground. Here is the one bag of money you gave me.' The master answered, 'You are a bad and lazy servant! You say you knew that I harvest what I did not plant and that I gather crops where I did not put any seed. So you should have put my money in the bank. Then, when I came home, I would get my money back. And I would also get the interest that my money earned.' So the master told his other servants, 'Take the one bag of money from that servant and give it to the servant who has ten bags. Everyone who uses what they have will get more. They will have much more than they need. But people who do not use what they have will have everything taken away from them" (Matthew 25:14–30, NIRV).

Yikes! This story is a great example of how God feels when we don't use the gifts He's given us. The master in the story called the servant who didn't use his talents a "bad and lazy servant." I don't know about you, but I don't want to be a "bad and lazy servant"! I want to be a good servant who works hard at my gifts. God gave us gifts to use…so we should use them to the best of our abilities.

Bazooka Boys ★ Who Am I?

How can we have self-control when it comes to our gifts? How can we make sure we're doing the hard work and being a faithful servant with our talents?

 # 1. DISCOVER YOUR GIFTS.

We've already learned EVERYONE has gifts from God. And we've learned that everyone's gifts are different from everyone else's. The first thing we should do to be faithful with our gifts is to discover what they are!

What are your gifts?

What are you good at?

What makes you happy?

What are some things that come really easy to you?

What kind of things do you like learning about?

What do you do for fun?

At the end of this lesson, we have a quiz that will help you figure it out. Take the quiz, make a list, or ask your friends and family what talents or gifts they see in you. They may have some great ideas!

Lucas didn't think he had any gifts. He didn't like to sing or play piano. He didn't like to draw or play soccer like his friends. He always thought gifts were just things you did in music or art class. But one day his mom commented on how God had given him the gift of compassion. He wasn't sure what that meant, so he asked his mom to explain. His mom said, "Someone with the gift of compassion notices when other people are sad and hurt and wants to help. You always think about other people and go out of your way to make sure they're okay. Not everyone thinks that way, Lucas. God made you especially sensitive to other people's feelings so you could reach out and help them. It's a special gift, and it is awesome!"

This was a such a cool moment for Lucas! As far back as he could remember, he had a heart for those who were hurting. It was never something he had to try to do—it was part of who he is.

For some reason, it had never occurred to him that this wasn't an accident. Part of God's design and plan for his life was a soft heart toward people!

This totally changed Lucas's life. From that moment on, he paid close attention when his heart was sad for another person. Instead of ignoring the feeling or simply brushing it off, he looked at it as a mission from heaven to reach out to the person God had put in his path.

Maybe your gift is that you care for people like Lucas. Maybe you're good at teaching other people. Maybe you're good at playing a certain sport or instrument. Maybe your gift is leading other people, or maybe you love to organize things.

The first way you can make sure you are using self-control with your gifts is to make sure you know what they are. Once you know what you're passionate about, the second thing you need to do is…

2. PRACTICE, PRACTICE, PRACTICE!

Jackson LOVES to play the violin. He started taking lessons when he was little, and he could tell right away that he's good at it. He didn't even have to try very hard when he first started. The music just flew right out of his fingers!

Then his teacher started giving him harder music to play, and he had to spend extra time practicing every day. Pretty soon, he started whining and complaining whenever it was time to practice. His mom got frustrated, and eventually Jackson would get to it, but he didn't have a very good attitude.

Jackson's story probably sounds familiar. A lot of us have talents that we're excited to use at first, but having natural talent is only the very beginning of

having gifts. We have to practice, learn, and study if we want to grow. That takes a lot of hard work and self-control.

Some of you are really gifted at something, but you've stopped working hard at growing in your gifts. You're not practicing hard. You're not studying. You're not working hard to get better. The truth is, when it comes to your talent, you'll only get out of it what you put into it. If you're not working at growing your gift, you'll stay at the level you've always been.

But if you practice hard, you'll get better. If you keep working every day, you'll grow stronger. You'll be like the servant in the story who pleased the Master because he worked hard to make sure he used what he'd been given and multiplied it into something more.

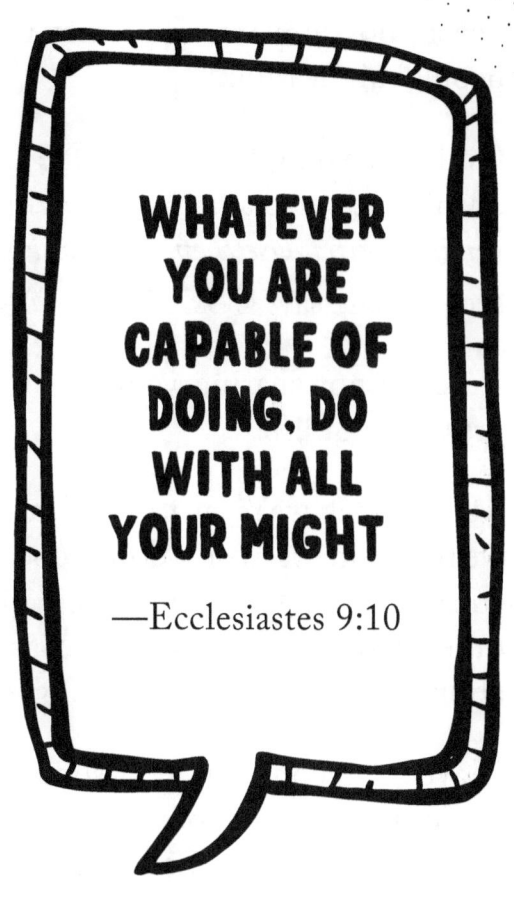

WHATEVER YOU ARE CAPABLE OF DOING, DO WITH ALL YOUR MIGHT

—Ecclesiastes 9:10

Ecclesiastes 9:10 says, "*Whatever you are capable of doing, do with all your might…*" That means you work your hardest. You practice every day. You go to classes and lessons and ask questions so you can get better.

So, we need to discover our gifts, practice hard, and lastly…

 ## 3. SHARE OUR GIFTS WITH OTHERS!

I think there are a lot of people in the world who **KNOW** what their gifts are, but they're too scared to **SHARE** their gifts with others. Maybe they love to sing but would **NEVER** sing in front of other people. Maybe they **LOVE** to play basketball in the yard with their family, but they're too nervous to join a team and play when other people are watching. Maybe they love to build things, but they never show anyone what they've made because they're scared of what other people might think.

God gave you gifts because He wants you to use them to help others! Look at our theme verse again: *"God has given each of you a gift from his great variety of spiritual gifts. Use them well to serve one another"* (1 Peter 4:10). What does that second part say? USE THEM WELL TO SERVE ONE ANOTHER!

If you're not sharing your gifts with others, you're missing out on one of the great joys of life!

Many times we're just scared to use our gifts. We don't want to look silly, or we're afraid we won't do a good job. Remember the third servant in the our story in Matthew? He hid his gift! He said, "I was afraid." He was afraid of other people's reactions. He was afraid of failing. He was unsure of his own abilities. He just stopped trying.

Maybe someone has said something mean to you or made fun of you when you've tried to use your gift in the past. Sometimes it can be hard to get past a bad experience. Maybe someone has mistreated your gift.

I know this can be so hard, but don't fall for it! Don't allow someone else to keep you from what God has for you. Even if it's scary, remind yourself that God has plans for you and your talents.

When I've faced this situation, it's helped me to refocus my attention away from what **OTHER** people think of me and determine that it is far more important for me to please my Heavenly Father than any other person. I remember Galatians 1:10: *"If I were still trying to please men, I would not be Christ's servant."* Do not allow another person to convince you that your gift has no value. Do not let your fear of what other people might say keep you sidelined. Decide to use

Bazooka Boys ★ Who Am I?

your talents as a faithful servant of Jesus, and let Him deal with the people who would try to discourage you.

If your gift is sitting on a shelf gathering dust, it's time to take it down and start using it again!

First Timothy 4:14–16 says, "*…that special gift of ministry you were given when the leaders of the church laid hands on you and prayed—keep that dusted off and in use. Cultivate these things. Immerse yourself in them. The people will all see you mature right before their eyes! Keep a firm grasp on both your character and your teaching. Don't be diverted. Just keep at it*" (MSG).

God has given you gifts. Discover what they are. Faithfully practice and grow them. Faithfully share them with others.

Bazooka Boys ★ Who Am I?

BIBLE BLITZ

PRACTICE MAKES PERFECT BASKETBALL SHOOT

(10 minutes)

Supplies

- Basket, trash can, or other type of container
- Small plastic balls (5 per team)
- Tape
- Numbered verse list

Prep

- Print off copies of the verse list.
- Create a throw line using tape or some other marker.
- Place basket a good distance away from the line.

Directions

1. Divide the boys into teams.

2. On their turn, the boys should throw the balls, attempting to get as many balls in the basket as possible.

3. When they finish their turn, each boy should run to the basket and count the number of balls that went in.

4. Have each boy read the scripture verse that matches the number of baskets they made. (Ex. 3 baskets made, read verse 3) For younger boys, you may need to read the verse and have them repeat after you.

5. When they're done reading, they should bring the balls back to the next person in line.

1. "GOD HAS GIVEN EACH OF YOU A GIFT FROM HIS GREAT VARIETY OF SPIRITUAL GIFTS. USE THEM WELL TO SERVE ONE ANOTHER." 1 Peter 4:10

2. "WHATEVER YOU ARE CAPABLE OF DOING, DO WITH ALL YOUR MIGHT…" Ecclesiastes 9:10

3. "FOR I CAN DO EVERYTHING THROUGH CHRIST, WHO GIVES ME STRENGTH." Philippians 4:13

4. "IF I WERE STILL TRYING TO PLEASE MEN, I WOULD NOT BE CHRIST'S SERVANT." Galatians 1:10

5. "…THAT SPECIAL GIFT OF MINISTRY YOU WERE GIVEN WHEN THE LEADERS OF THE CHURCH LAID HANDS ON YOU AND PRAYED—KEEP THAT DUSTED OFF AND IN USE." 1 Timothy 4:14

GOD'S GIFT BINGO

(20 minutes)

Supplies
- Copy paper
- Cardstock
- Gluesticks
- Scissors
- Candy to use as markers
- Container to hold drawing pieces

Prep
- Photocopy gift squares sheets onto copy paper (multiple copies of each sheet)
- Photocopy blank bingo cards onto cardstock (one for each boy)
- Precut the gift squares.
- Place one set of all the gift squares into a container for calling bingo.

Directions
1. Have each boy select 8 "gift squares" that represent something they are good at or interested in.
2. Glue their gift squares onto their bingo card.
3. Give each boy candy to use as markers.
4. Have each player put a marker on their free space.
5. Have the leader draw from the gift squares container and call out the gift. Boys can mark their bingo card when their "gift" is called.
6. Any player that get 3 in a row (horizontal, vertical, or diagonal) calls Bingo and gets to eat their candy!
7. Continue game until all players have achieved bingo!

GOD'S GIFT BINGO

ASK THIS ★ REPEAT THIS ★ PRAY THIS ★ DOODLE THIS
(10 minutes)

Huddle up with your team just before you dismiss.

Ask This:

1. Where do our gifts come from? Does everyone have one?

2. Share one thing you're good at. Maybe it's a talent, a sport, a hobby, something at school, or even something about your personality that's unique and brings you or others joy.

3. What are some ways we can grow in our gifts? (*Possible Answers: Practice every day. Study—learn more. Ask people who are good at your talent to show you how to get better. Keep looking for opportunities to learn more about your talents.*)

Repeat This:

"God has given each of you a gift from his great variety of spiritual gifts. Use them well to serve one another." —1 Peter 4:10

Pray This:

"Dear God, Thank you for giving me gifts. I want to use them to the best of my ability. Help me work hard and get better. I want to use my gifts to show others how good you are. Amen."

Doodle This:

Have the boys turn to the Doodle page in their workbook (or copy it for them).

PARENT CONNECTION

One of the most enjoyable things about parenting is discovering your kids' unique gifts and talents. There's nothing more fun than watching them unearth their passions and seeing them excel in their own unique ways.

One of the most challenging things in parenting is learning how to help your child embrace their own gifts without comparing themselves to others. Sometimes our kids may not even realize the ways God has uniquely designed them to impact the world. Keep your eyes open for areas of passion and interest in your child and do everything you can to encourage them in these areas.

Having self-control when it comes to your gifts is a very important aspect of growth. There are many talented people who never measure up to their full potential because they lack the discipline to develop their natural abilities through hard work and practice. This week, we encouraged the boys to work diligently at their gifts and talents. Even when it's hard, we need to recognize that God has given us gifts for a purpose. It's our responsibility to use them to the best of our ability.

It's not enough to just know what our talents are—God wants us to USE them! There are so many gifted people in the world who aren't using the gifts God has given them. Encourage your sons to overcome fear and worry of what others will think and bravely use her talents.

We reminded the boys of Philippians 4:13: "*I can do everything through Christ, who gives me strength.*" Remind your son that, even if he's scared, God will help him do his very best!

DOODLE PAGE

LESSON 6

Everyone has gifts! In the boxes below, write out (or draw a picture of) 3 things that you are good at. Then in the boxes underneath, write out one way you can work hard to use that gift!

Bazooka Boys ★ Who Am I?

KINDERGARTEN AND 1ST GRADE

Our theme verse is 1 Peter 4:10. In the blank, fill in the word GIFTS!

"God has given each of you a gift from his great variety of spiritual _____. Use them well to serve one another." –1 Peter 4:10

Fill in the blanks to help discover your gifts and talents.

If I have an afternoon to myself, I love to _____.

My favorite subject in school is _____.

If I could volunteer to help somewhere, I would choose to help with _____.

I love to _____.

I want to learn more about _____.

My favorite hobbies are _____.

I'm happiest when I'm _____.

People say that I'm _____.

I feel really proud when I'm _____.

Draw a picture of you doing your favorite thing.

Bazooka Boys ★ Who Am I?

TAKE HOME ACTIVITY

2ND AND 3RD GRADE

Look up 1 Peter 4:10 in your Bible and write it in the space provided.

Fill in the blanks to help discover your gifts and talents.

If I have an afternoon to myself, I love to _____.

My favorite subject in school is _____.

If I could volunteer to help somewhere, I would choose to help with _____.

I love to _____.

I want to learn more about _____.

My favorite hobbies are _____.

I'm happiest when I'm _____.

People say that I'm _____.

I feel really proud when I'm _____.

WEEK 6

Here's a list of some gifts and talents. Circle anything you're good at.

Being kind

Caring about other people

Movies
(reviewing, writing, filming, story, acting)

Photography

Author (writing stories or articles)

Technology
(setting up blogs, fixing computers)

Thinking
(arguing, debating, worldview, philosophy)

Politics and government

Being responsible

Friendship

Helping your family or teachers

Taking care of God's creation

Telling others about Jesus

Starting new things

Memorizing things

Music

Sports

School

Science

Reading

Inventing

Listening to other people's problems

Visiting people who are sick or sad

Doing thoughtful things for others

Building things

Smiling

Going on adventures

Acting or drama

Art (drawing, painting, making)

Board games, strategy games

Building, construction, carpentry

Organizing things

Solving puzzles and mysteries

Leading a group

Giving things to others

Sharing

Praying for others

Studying the Bible

Teaching

Cooking

Crafts

Electronics
(computers, coding, video games)

Fashion design, sewing

Gardening (veggies, herbs, flowers)

Graphics Arts
(typography, Illustrator, Photoshop)

House renovations and maintenance

Interior decorating

Mechanics
(small motors, fixing things)

Bazooka Boys ★ Who Am I?

WEEK 6

Of the things you circled, write your three **FAVORITES** below:

1.

2.

3.

Bazooka Boys ★ Who Am I?

4TH AND 5TH GRADE

Look up 1 Peter 4:10 in your Bible and write it in the space provided.

Fill in the blanks to help discover your gifts and talents.

If I have an afternoon to myself, I love to _____.

My favorite subject in school is _____.

If I could volunteer to help somewhere, I would choose to help with _____.

I love to _____.

I want to learn more about _____.

My favorite hobbies are _____.

I'm happiest when I'm _____.

People say that I'm _____.

I feel really proud when I'm _____.

Here's a list of some gifts and talents. Circle anything you're good at.

Being kind

Caring about other people

Movies
(reviewing, writing, filming, story, acting)

Photography

Author (writing stories or articles)

Technology
(setting up blogs, fixing computers)

Thinking
(arguing, debating, worldview, philosophy)

Politics and government

Being responsible

Friendship

Helping your family or teachers

Taking care of God's creation

Telling others about Jesus

Starting new things

Memorizing things

Music

Sports

School

Science

Reading

Inventing

Listening to other people's problems

Visiting people who are sick or sad

Doing thoughtful things for others

Building things

Smiling

Going on adventures

Acting or drama

Art (drawing, painting, making)

Board games, strategy games

Building, construction, carpentry

Organizing things

Solving puzzles and mysteries

Leading a group

Giving things to others

Sharing

Praying for others

Studying the Bible

Teaching

Cooking

Crafts

Electronics
(computers, coding, video games)

Fashion design, sewing

Gardening (veggies, herbs, flowers)

Graphics Arts
(typography, Illustrator, Photoshop)

House renovations and maintenance

Interior decorating

Mechanics
(small motors, fixing things)

Bazooka Boys ★ Who Am I?

Of the things you circled, write your three FAVORITES below:

1.

2.

3.

In the space provided, write out three things you can do to get better at your gifts.

1.

2.

3.

What are three ways you could start using your gifts RIGHt NOW?

BAZOOKA BLAST OVERVIEW: WEEK 7

Large Group Lesson: *(15 minutes)*
- We all have the same amount of minutes everyday and God wants us to use them well!
- We need to practice self-control in our work time by doing well at school, our extra activities, and other responsibilities.
- We need to practice self-control in our play time by being wise about screen time and honor the limits our parents set.
- We need to practice self-control in our rest time by honoring a Sabbath and making sure we get plenty of sleep!

Bazooka Blitz: Small Group Time:

Bible Blitz *(10 minutes)*
  Work/Play/Rest Relay *(Instructions on page 171)*

Bazooka Project *(20 minutes)*
  Taking My Time Doorhanger *(Instructions on page 173)*

Team Huddle *(10 minutes)*

Ask This:
1. What is your WORK? In other words, what are the responsibilities you have every day? (*School, chores, practice, lessons, etc*) What are some ways you can have more self-control in your work?
2. When it comes to your playtime, what is the thing that is hardest for you to practice self-control? What can you do to be better about limits during your playtime?
3. What is a Sabbath? What are some ways you can be sure to rest every week?

Repeat This: "*There is a right time for everything...*"
—Ecclesiastes 3:1 (ERV)

Pray This: "*Dear God, I want to be wise using the time you've given me each day. Help me to do a good job with my worktime. Show me how to have good self-control in my playtime. And help me find time to rest so I can do my very best for you. Amen.*"

Doodle This: Have the boys turn to the Doodle page in their workbook (or copy it for them).

Bazooka Boys ★ Who Am I?

TAKING MY TIME

What's the Point?
God wants us to be smart about how we use our time.

THEME VERSE
There is a right time for everything…
Ecclesiastes 3:1 (ERV)

RELATED BIBLE PASSAGE
Daniel 1:17–21

★ LARGE GROUP LESSON ★
(15 minutes)

Do you know how many hours are in a day? **24**.

Do you know how many minutes are in a day? **1,440**.

Do you know how many seconds are in a day? **86,400**.

When God made the world, He started **TIME**. He caused the sun to rise in the morning and set in the evening, created morning and night, and gave us days and weeks and years. **TIME** is something God created.

He gives each and every one of us the same amount of hours, minutes, and seconds in a day. No one gets more. No one gets less. You can't buy more hours for your day.

God wants us to be smart about how we use the time He has given us. Psalm 90:12 says, *"Teach us to number our days, that we may gain a heart of wisdom."* God wants us to realize that every day is precious and we need to make good use of the time He has given us.

God has a plan for every single day of your life. Not one day is wasted. There's not one day that's unimportant. Psalm 139:16 says, *"Every day of my life was recorded in Your book. Every moment was laid out before a single day had passed."* Every day is important and filled with things God has planned for you to do!

So **WHY** is it so easy to manage our time poorly?

WHY do we sometimes waste too much time on things that aren't important?

WHY do we sometimes waste time doing the things we know we shouldn't be doing?

Bazooka Boys ★ Who Am I?

Andrew was having a hard time managing his time. Most of his days looked like this: His Mom would wake him up for school, but he would have a hard time getting up. (He had stayed up extra late the night before playing video games, so he was just **SO** tired!) He would lie in bed until he was late and his Mom would yell at him from the kitchen. He would race out of bed, grab some dirty, wrinkly clothes, and race down to breakfast. After he ate, he would run to put his lunch in his backpack and realize he had forgotten to do yesterday's homework assignment! He had meant to do it, but when he got home, he got distracted by his iPad and never got back to it. Oops.

As Andrew raced onto the bus, he wasn't feeling very good about himself. Why was he always forgetting things? Why was he always late? Why couldn't he get his act together?

The truth is, that Andrew was not practicing self-control when it came to his time. He wasn't making good choices about how he spent his minutes. He just went with whatever he felt like doing in the moment instead of making decisions based on what was the best use of his time. He needed to make a plan to manage his time better and then stick to it!

God wants us to be wise with the time He has given us every day. Here are three places we need to have self-control with our time.

 ## 1. HAVE SELF-CONTROL IN YOUR WORK TIME.

Do you have a job? I'm guessing that none of you get up in the morning, put on a suit and grab a briefcase, and head out to work! But you **DO** have work that you are responsible for every single day—going to school and doing your very best with your studies, chores and responsibilities at home, things you're committed to (sports teams, music lessons, other clubs or classes).

The first and most important area where you learn to manage your time well is your work. God wants you to be a hard worker. Colossians 3:23 says, "*In all the work you are given, do the best you can. Work as though you are working for the Lord, not any earthly master."* (ERV).

God wants you to work hard! He wants you to do your very best. He wants you to be dependable and responsible. There are lots of reasons this is important, but do you know one of the most important reasons you should be self-controlled with your time? It's is a great way to show others you love Jesus!

There's a story in the Bible about a boy named Daniel and his friends, who were captured and taken to Babylon to be put in the king's service. Everyone watched to see how these four young men would handle this tough situation. This is what the Bible says about Daniel and his friends:

"Every time the king asked them about something important, they showed great wisdom and understanding. The king found they were ten times better than all the magicians and wise men in his kingdom" (Daniel 1:20, ERV).

The King and all the other people in the kingdom took note that Daniel and his friends were smart, helpful, and worked hard. It didn't matter what kind of situation they were in, they determined to do their very best no matter what.

My prayer is that any teacher, coach, or friend you have contact with finds you ten times better than anyone else around—just like Daniel! When they ask you why, you'll be able to share that you work hard because you love God and the Bible tells you to!

A lot of people WANT to be ten times better at stuff, but they're not willing to do the hard work to get there. Proverbs 13:4 says, *"Lazy*

Bazooka Boys ★ Who Am I?

people always want things but never get them. Those who work hard get plenty" (ERV). So make sure you're studying hard. Make sure you're practicing what you're supposed to be practicing. Make sure you show up on time and don't skip out on things you've committed to.

Determine to be a hard worker today! Show up on time. Get your homework done. Make sure you do your chores well, and without complaining. Be a good manager of your time.

 2. HAVE SELF-CONTROL IN YOUR PLAY TIME.

Ben was so excited for Saturday, he could hardly wait! He had a long week at school with so much homework that he couldn't wait to have a day off. He started a marathon of one of his favorite games on his computer, and he just kept playing and playing and playing. After a while, he started feeling kind of yucky. His muscles were feeling sore and he was feeling super blah. His mom came upstairs and asked him how long he had been playing his game, and Ben realized it had been four hours! His mom was not very happy with him, and he was not very happy with himself, either.

How many of you have limits on your computer or iPad time? How many of you have rules about how much TV you can watch? How many of you have rules about how many video games you can play? Why do you think your parents give you rules like that?

It's not good for us to spend too much time doing those things. It's super fun to be able to play fun games and watch good movies or TV shows, but many of us have a hard time practicing self-control. Sometimes we do it as **LONG** as we can get away with (before our parents realize what we've been

> "LAZY PEOPLE ALWAYS WANT THINGS BUT NEVER GET THEM. THOSE WHO WORK HARD GET PLENTY"
> –Proverbs 13:4 (ERV)

doing), but I want to challenge you—**YOU** are supposed to be the one who shows self-control with your time. **YOU** are in charge of the minutes God has given you. Instead of just trying to get away with as much as you can get away with, think about what a healthy time limit is and talk about it with your parents. Then **YOU** take responsibility for staying within those time limits. Maybe you need to set a timer for yourself. Maybe you need to commit to watching one episode of something at a time instead of watching 25!

One of the **BIGGEST** ways you can practice self-control is by making good choices in how you handle your play time!

And the last way you can practice self-control with your time is to…

 ## 3. HAVE SELF-CONTROL IN YOUR REST TIME.

Have you ever thought about how weird it is that we all **SLEEP** every night? It gets dark outside, we all go into our rooms and crawl into bed, and we pretty much don't know what's going on around us for eight or nine hours. It's weird!

But God designed our bodies to need sleep and God designed our bodies to need rest! If our bodies and minds don't have time to just check out and recover, pretty soon they start wearing down and getting sick. So we need to practice self-control in how we rest!

That means you need to make sure you're getting enough sleep! Remember our story about Andrew, who had such a hard time getting out of bed? Part of his problem was that he wasn't making good choices about getting enough sleep so he could work hard the next day. He was simply doing what he wanted to do at the moment without thinking about how it would affect his ability to do his best at school the next day. (Hmm…Do you remember learning about "I want what I want when I want it"? Seems like Andrew needs to push down the flesh and have self-control!) God wants you to do your best every day. That starts with doing your best to get a good night's sleep.

Bazooka Boys ★ Who Am I?

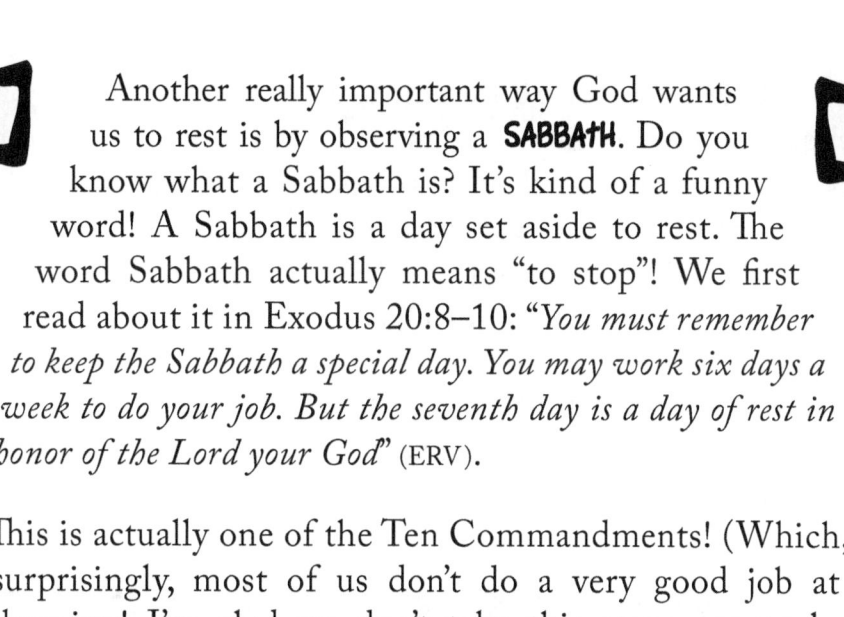

Another really important way God wants us to rest is by observing a **SABBATH**. Do you know what a Sabbath is? It's kind of a funny word! A Sabbath is a day set aside to rest. The word Sabbath actually means "to stop"! We first read about it in Exodus 20:8–10: *"You must remember to keep the Sabbath a special day. You may work six days a week to do your job. But the seventh day is a day of rest in honor of the Lord your God"* (ERV).

This is actually one of the Ten Commandments! (Which, surprisingly, most of us don't do a very good job at keeping! I'm glad we don't take this same approach with "thou shall not kill!")

Basically, a Sabbath is a day when we take the time to rest and worship. We step away from our normal routine and allow ourselves time to reflect, connect with our families, and rest our bodies.

The Bible is very clear that you and I should set aside time every single week for **REST**. Now, resting might mean taking a nice long nap for some of us, but resting can mean a whole lot of other things, too. You can rest by going for a nice walk with your family. You can rest by cooking a meal or playing a game. You can rest by reading a book or throwing around a baseball. Resting means doing something you enjoy in a relaxed environment. Think about what makes you feel refreshed and ready to take on another day. Whatever those things are, you should make sure you take the time to do those things once a week.

At our house, we have a Sabbath on most Sundays. When we wake up, we have a family rule that no one uses electronics for the morning. This is just something we do to remind us that it's a day to rest and do things differently. Then we go to church and spend time learning about God. Then we try and have a family meal together to talk about the next week and all that's coming up. Then we each do some things that we personally enjoy.

Everybody's Sabbath may look different. Your family may have a Saturday night Sabbath where you have family time and rest. Maybe you have some quiet time during another part of the week. Talk to your parents about ways you can plan some rest time into your family routine every week. God wants to take good care of us, and He tells us over and over in the Bible that we should make sure we have self-control when it comes to having times of rest!

God wants you to have discipline when it comes to your time. Whether you're at work, at play, or at rest, do your very best with the time God has given you every single day!

WORK/PLAY/REST RELAY

(10 minutes)

Supplies

- Blocks (10 per team)
- Small plastic balls (10 per team)
- Baskets or buckets (1 per team)
- Sleeping bag or blankets (1 per team)
- Teddy bear or other stuffed animal (1 per team)

Prep

- Set up 3 stations for each team.
- Station 1 is the **WORK** station where the boys will need to stack 10 blocks.
- Station 2 is the **PLAY** station where they will need to throw 10 balls into the baskets.
- Station 3 is the **REST** station where the boys will need to crawl into the sleeping bag, snuggle the teddy bear and snore 5 times.

Directions

1. Divide the boys into teams.
2. When you say go, each boy needs to run to each station and accomplish the task.
3. After he finishes the work, play, and rest tasks, he tags the next boy in line.
4. First team to finish wins!

Bazooka Boys ★ Who Am I?

TAKING MY TIME DOORHANGER

(20 minutes)

Supplies

- Foam Door Hanger
- Permanent Markers (variety of colors)
- Wooden Clothes Pins (5 or 6 per boy)
- Foam Stickers (optional)

Directions

1. Use a permanent marker to write on the foam door hanger:
   – Write "**TO DO**" on the left side under the opening.
   – Write "**DONE**" on the right side under the opening.

2. Use a permanent marker to write different types of chores on each clothes pin (brush teeth, make bed, take out garbage, load dishes, unload dishes, read, etc.).

3. Decorate the door hanger with foam stickers (optional).

4. Have the boys put the doorhanger in a place they will see it every day. Once they've completed their chores, move the clothes pin from the "To Do" side to the "Done" side.

Bazooka Boys ★ Who Am I?

ASK THIS ★ REPEAT THIS ★ PRAY THIS ★ DOODLE THIS
(10 minutes)

Huddle up with your team just before you dismiss.

Ask This:

1. What is your **WORK**? In other words, what are the responsibilities you have every day? (*School, chores, practice, lessons, etc*) What are some ways you can have more self-control in your work?

2. When it comes to your playtime, what is the thing that is hardest for you to practice self-control? What can you do to be better about limits during your playtime?

3. What is a Sabbath? What are some ways you can be sure to rest every week?

Repeat This:

"There is a right time for everything..." —Ecclesiastes 3:1 (ERV)

Pray This:

"Dear God, I want to be wise using the time you've given me each day. Help me to do a good job with my worktime. Show me how to have good self-control in my playtime. And help me find time to rest so I can do my very best for you. Amen."

Doodle This:

Have the boys turn to the Doodle page in their workbook (or copy it for them).

PARENT CONNECTION

Most days I struggle to manage my time well. I'm guessing some of you do, too. Kids are no different. As we look at practicing self-control in every area of our lives, this is certainly an area where we need all the help we can get!

Colossians 3:23 says, *"In all the work you are given, do the best you can. Work as though you are working for the Lord, not an earthly master"* (ERV). We encouraged the boys to practice discipline when it comes to their work time—school, homework, chores, extra curricular activities. They learned that making wise choices with their time and work ethic will help them stand out from the crowd and show people they love Jesus.

Second, we challenged the kids to practice self-control in their play time. We all know the battle of getting our kids to regulate their screen time! We challenged the boys to take responsibility for a balanced approach to play time rather than trying to get away with as much as they can.

Last, we taught the boys about getting adequate rest and honoring a Sabbath. Many of our kids have no idea how to actually rest and allow their bodies and minds to be replenished. You can set the example for your kids by showing them what a balanced life looks like. Make sure you're intentional about seasons of rest for your family. It's a lifelong lesson they will thank you for someday!

DOODLE PAGE
LESSON 7

Write a list or draw a picture of 3 things you need to do today.

Write a list or draw a picture of 3 things you want to do today.

Number your items in the order in which you should do them.

Bazooka Boys ★ Who Am I?

TAKE HOME ACTIVITY

KINDERGARTEN AND 1ST GRADE

On the clock below, draw a picture or write a list of some things you do for your work time, play time, and rest time every day.

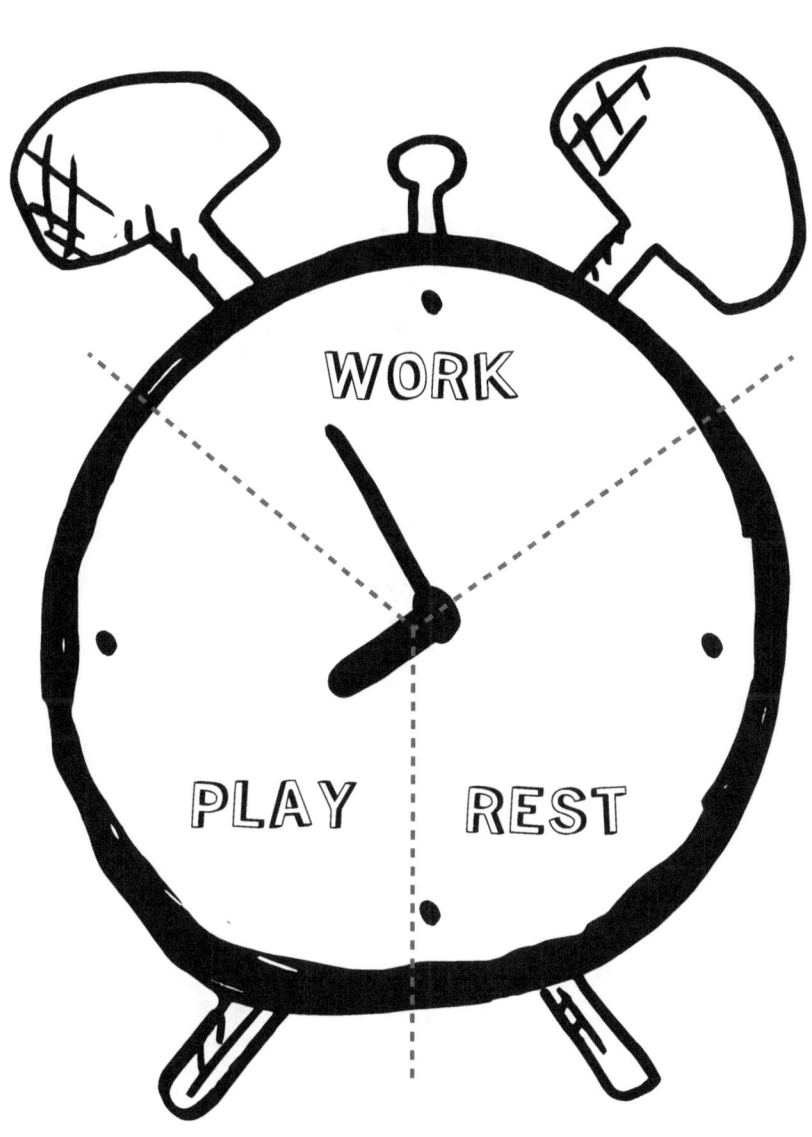

Find the words in the puzzle!

```
Q K P X S U R K F
H C G L L R I G Y
P O T L A Z U Z O
S L L U T Y I O A
A C H W O R K F H
D N N E V V F I Z
X U M L D G P W V
P I M R J J I A U
T S O N B D Z M M
```

WORD LIST

Clock

Hours

Play

Time

Work

Bazooka Boys ★ Who Am I?

 TAKE HOME ACTIVITY

2ND AND 3RD GRADE

On the clock below, draw a picture or write a list of some things you do for your work time, play time, and rest time every day.

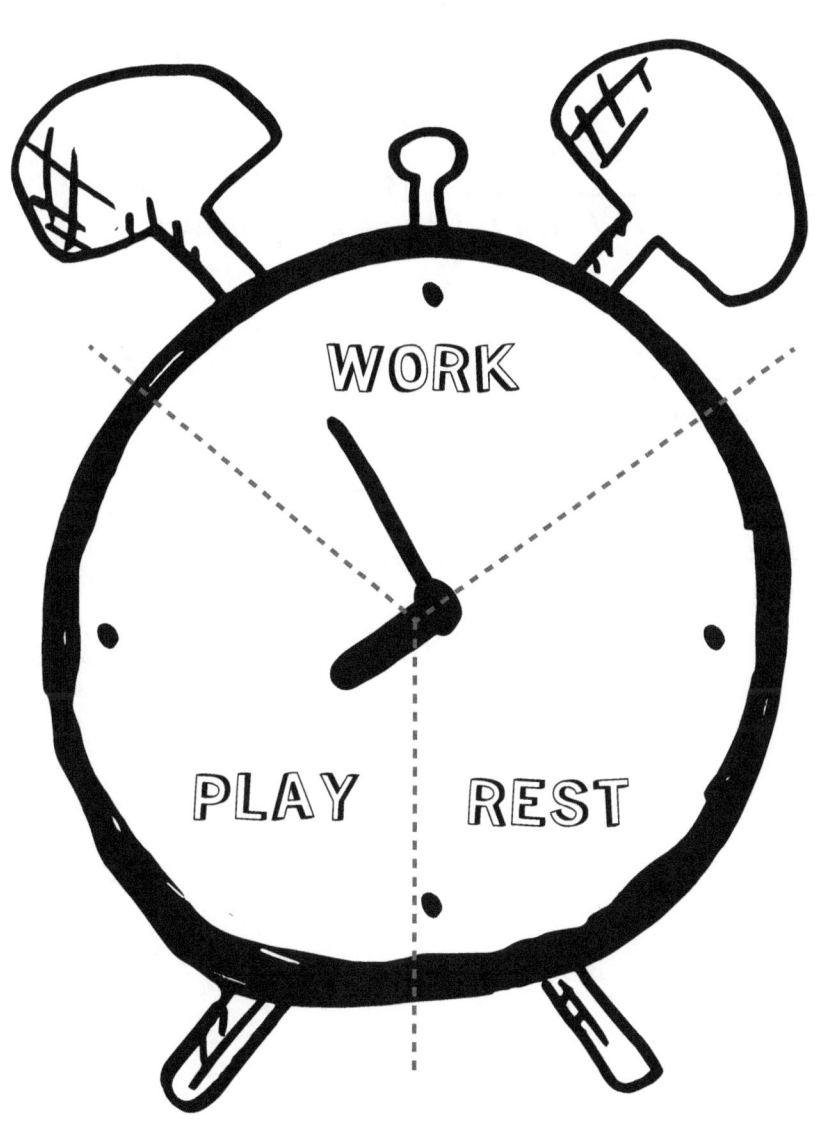

Use the word list below to fill in the blanks and complete these verses.

Psalm 139:16

Every _____ of my life was recorded in Your book.

Every _____ was laid out before a single had passed.

Ecclesiastes 3:1

There is a right _____ for everything.

Psalm 90:12

Teach us to number our days that we may gain a heart of _____.

Colossians 3:23

In all the _____ you are given, do the best you can. Work as though you are working for the Lord, not any earthly master.

Proverbs 13:4

_____ people always want things but never get them. Those who work hard get plenty.

Exodus 20:8

You must remember to keep the _____ as a special day.

Word List:

Sabbath

Time

Day

Lazy

Wisdom

Work

Day

Bazooka Boys ★ Who Am I?

Find the words in the puzzle below!

```
V S M Z P Y E C T T H C Y V S
M R P T I M Z K X H H K A P Z
R T D Q X T P A E U T A D D Z
H O U R S N O R L X A H Y U F
T O F H J I G J C R B T K K N
Z P L U H S M Z E W B P B U Q
S R I G S M W C X T A Y A L P
P O V J Z Y B V N V S L V H N
R R I U W J U Z N P P I V H M
C D E Y A O B Y F Y Q M Y O V
W L G W P H T O H J S G D R F
I A O P Z T I Y L S T S N J M
J R K C U A M F N R I D D G I
K X X Z K F E J L W V L L B T
V C Z R A P I E A I D C V P N
```

Word List:

Clock

Day

Hours

Lazy

Play

Sabbath

Time

Wisdom

Work

183

Bazooka Boys ★ Who Am I?

4TH AND 5TH GRADE

Use the word list below to fill in the blanks and complete these verses.

Psalm 139:16

Every _____ of my life was recorded in Your book.

Every _____ was laid out before a single had passed.

Ecclesiastes 3:1

There is a right _____ for everything.

Psalm 90:12

Teach us to number our days that we may gain a heart of _____.

Colossians 3:23

In all the _____ you are given, do the best you can. Work as though you are working for the Lord, not any earthly master.

Proverbs 13:4

_____ people always want things but never get them. Those who work hard get plenty.

Exodus 20:8

You must remember to keep the _____ as a special day.

Word List:

Sabbath *Lazy* *Day*

Time *Wisdom*

Day *Work*

Find the words in the puzzle below!

```
V S M Z P Y E C T T H C Y V S
M R P T I M Z K X H H K A P Z
R T D Q X T P A E U T A D D Z
H O U R S N O R L X A H Y U F
T O F H J I G J C R B T K K N
Z P L U H S M Z E W B P B U Q
S R I G S M W C X T A Y A L P
P O V J Z Y B V N V S L V H N
R R I U W J U Z N P P I V H M
C D E Y A O B Y F Y Q M Y O V
W L G W P H T O H J S G D R F
I A O P Z T I Y L S T S N J M
J R K C U A M F N R I D D G I
K X X Z K F E J L W V L L B T
V C Z R A P I E A I D C V P N
```

Word List:

Clock

Day

Hours

Lazy

Play

Sabbath

Time

Wisdom

Work

Bazooka Boys ★ Who Am I?

Read the story of Daniel in Daniel 1. In the blanks below, write three things Daniel did that set him apart from all the other people.

1. _____

2. _____

3. _____

What can you learn from Daniel's example?

BAZOOKA BLAST OVERVIEW: WEEK 8

Large Group Lesson: *(15 minutes)*

- Obedience is very important to God. We need to obey God and those He has put in authority over us.
- We should obey without delay—as soon as we are asked to do something.
- God wants us to obey all the way—making sure we follow through with all the things we've been asked to do.
- Obeying the right way means we have a good attitude while we're obeying!

Bazooka Blitz: Small Group Time:

Bible Blitz *(15 minutes)*
Obey Stacking Contest *(Instructions on page 197)*

Bazooka Project *(20 minutes)*
"Do What I Say" Maze Challenge *(Instructions on page 199)*

Team Huddle *(10 minutes)*

Ask This:

1. God wants us to obey without delay. Give an example of a time when you didn't obey right away.
2. When we're asked to do something by someone in authority over us, is it okay to only obey part of their instructions? Why is this important?
3. We need to obey with a good attitude. Share a time when you did something you weren't really excited about, but you did it with a good attitude anyway.

Repeat This: *"Children, obey your parents the way the Lord wants, because this is the right thing to do."* —Ephesians 6:1 (ERV)

Pray This: *"Dear Jesus, I know that you want me to obey my parents and those in authority. Forgive me for not obeying right away, all the way, and the right way. Help me to do better. Amen."*

Doodle This: Have the boys turn to the Doodle page in their workbook (or copy it for them).

THE WAY TO OBEY

WHAT'S THE POINT?
God wants us to obey, without delay, all the way, the right way!

THEME VERSE

Children, obey your parents the way the Lord wants, because this is the right thing to do.
Ephesians 6:1 (ERV)

RELATED BIBLE PASSAGE

Numbers 20:1–13

★ LARGE GROUP LESSON ★
(15 minutes)

Have you ever played "Simon Says?" You know, the game where the leader tells you what to do and you have to do whatever they say? It's such a fun game to play, especially if you get to be the one telling everyone what to do. **OH, THE POWER!** Mwahhhhhhhhaaaa! (Insert evil laugh here.) It's fun to be in charge of other people!

It's super fun to be the leader in "Simon Says," and it's still kind of fun to be the one following directions. But it isn't always fun to have to do what other people tell you to do in real life. Like when your mom tells you to do your homework before playing with your friends (ugh!). Or when your teacher tells you to stop talking to your neighbor and finish your assignment (double ugh!). Or when your dad tells you to organize the garage while your friends are all going to the movies (triple super-duper ugh!).

God puts people in our lives who are kind of the boss of us while we're young. Romans 13:1 says, *"For all authority comes from God, and those in positions of authority have been placed there by God"*. These people have been put in authority by God to take care of us and help us grow. They keep us safe and teach us how to become good, responsible people. These people are your parents, teachers, leaders, pastors, coaches, and others in positions of authority over you. God

"FOR ALL AUTHORITY COMES FROM GOD, AND THOSE IN POSITIONS OF AUTHORITY HAVE BEEN PLACED THERE BY GOD."

wants us to honor them in many ways, including speaking respectfully, listening to what they say, and most importantly, obeying them.

OBEY—that's kind of a funny word, isn't it? Do you know what it means? It means to do whatever someone in authority over you tells you to do. It means to follow their instructions or commands. It means listening to directions and following those directions.

It's very important to remember that, first and foremost, God wants us to obey Him. He has given us instructions in the Bible, and it matters a lot to Him that we obey those instructions. Jeremiah 42:6 says, *"Whether we like it or not, we will obey the Lord our God to whom we are sending you with our plea. For if we obey him, everything will turn out well for us"*. Sometimes we may not want to do the right thing, but this verse reminds us that when we choose to do the things God has told us to do (and when we choose **NOT** to do the things God has told us **NOT** to do), things will go well for us. If we choose to disobey God, we're going to have some problems and things will not go well for us. But if we follow His instructions, He has promised to lead us on the best possible path for our lives!

God wants us to obey Him, and He wants us to obey the authority figures He has put in our lives. Ephesians 6:1 tells us, *"Children, obey your parents the way the Lord wants, because this is the right thing to do"* (ERV). Obeying your parents, teachers, and leaders is an important part of growing up and honoring God with your life.

THAT'S NOT ALWAYS EASY, IS IT?

Sometimes we just don't feel like doing what we've been told to do. Sometimes we don't like the instructions we've been given. Sometimes we're just lazy or want to do things our own way. Obedience might seem like a simple idea, but it's certainly not easy!

If we want to honor God, we need to learn to obey. So here are three ways we can honor God with our obedience.

The first way, is to...

1. OBEY WITHOUT DELAY.

When Dalton got home from school one day, he was exhausted. He dropped his coat and backpack on the floor in the hallway and ran to the kitchen to grab a granola bar and juice box. His mom yelled down the stairs, "Dalton! Make sure you hang up your coat and backpack!"

Dalton yelled back, "Okay," but he was digging through the box for his favorite flavor of juice box and was distracted by all the yumminess. Once he found just the right beverage, he remembered he wanted to check his iPad to see if there was a message from his friend about meeting at the park, so he ran to the desk when he heard his mom yell down the stairs again, "Dalton, did you hang up your coat and backpack?" He yelled back, "Just a minute!" as he scrolled through his messages looking for a reply. He really intended to go hang up his backpack just as soon as he replied to his friend, but he remembered that he was in the middle of a super awesome game and was **JUST** about to finish a level, so he sat down and started playing.

A few minutes later, he looked up to see his mom standing in front of him with a not-so-happy look on her face. "Dalton! I told you to pick up your coat and backpack!" Dalton, suddenly remembered what he was supposed to do and felt bad that he hadn't obeyed his mother right away. He meant to do it, but he got distracted and ended up disobeying what his mother had said to do.

When our parents, teachers, or coaches ask us to do something, we need to obey **RIGHT THEN**. It's not okay to say, "I'll eventually get to it," or "I'll do it later!" That is not obeying. It's also not okay to ignore someone when they're giving you instructions or put off doing the thing they tell you to do. Being obedient means immediately doing the thing being asked of us, not waiting until later,

not getting around to it eventually, not ignoring instructions. It means obeying without delay.

Most importantly, it's important to quickly obey God when He tells you to do something. Psalm 119:60 says, "*I won't waste any time. I will be quick to obey your commands*" (NIRV). Obeying God and others immediately is the only way to obey.

The second way we can honor God with our obedience is to…

 **2. OBEY ALL tHE WAY.**

Have your parents ever told you to clean up your room? Then when you walk in, you realize what a total disaster it is and instead of actually picking up the toys and clothes, you simply shove everything into the closet or under the bed? Is that really obeying what your parents have told you to do? I don't think so.

Obeying means you do what has been asked of you completely. You do exactly what you have been told to do, and you do a good job. Doing something half way isn't obedience.

There's a story in the Bible that shows how God feels about half-way obedience. Moses led the Israelites out of Egypt, and now they were wandering around in the wilderness. It was hot, and they were thirsty! Moses and his brother Aaron prayed and asked God to miraculously provide something for the people to drink. God told Moses to speak to a rock, and then water would flow out of it. (Umm…super cool!)

When Moses got to the rock, he didn't follow God's instructions. He was frustrated with the people and all their grumbling and complaining. Instead of speaking to the rock like God told him to, he hit it with his staff instead. Now, God didn't want to see His people die of thirst, so He caused water to come out of the rock anyway.

But God was not very happy with Moses and Aaron. Numbers 20:12 says, "*God said to Moses and Aaron, 'Because you didn't trust me, didn't treat me with holy reverence in front of the People of Israel, you two aren't going to lead this company into the land that I am giving them.'*" God punished them for not doing exactly what He had told them to do. Not only did they strike the rock instead of speaking to it, they didn't remind the people that the miracle came from God, and they took the glory of the miracle for themselves. Because of their disobedience, they were not able to enter the Promised Land. They were punished because they didn't obey God all the way.

When God asks you to do something, do it until it's complete. When your parents tell you something, follow their instructions. When your teachers or coaches give you directions, do your very best to do what they say. Don't do things halfway—obey all the way.

The last way we can honor God with our obedience is to…

 ## 3. OBEY THE RIGHT WAY.

All of us have been asked to do things that we REALLY don't want to do. We already talked about the idea that God wants us to obey, all the way, without delay. It's also important to obey with a good attitude and good effort.

Sometimes that can be really hard! Maybe your mom told you to clean your room and you obeyed her, but the whole time you were cleaning you stomped your feet and slammed doors. Or maybe you complained and whined the whole time. Or maybe you did the job as slow as possible just because you were trying to make sure everyone knew how UNHAPPY you were that you had to clean your room.

Do you think obeying with a bad attitude is pleasing to God? I don't think so. Of course it's important to follow through even when you don't feel like it, but it's also important to obey with the right heart and actions.

Bazooka Boys ★ Who Am I?

Philippians 2:14 says, *"Do everything without complaining or arguing."* (NIRV). We need to check our attitude while we're obeying. Are we "technically" obeying while throwing a fit? Or, are we working with a good attitude even if it's not our favorite thing to do? God honors a good attitude because it's a sign of respect to those He has put in charge of us.

One last thought about obeying: God wants you to obey your earthly authority, but He wants you to obey His Word first and foremost. If you ever have an authority in your life wanting you to do or say something that goes against God's laws, you need to talk to a trusted adult about the situation. Sometimes adults make mistakes too, and God doesn't want you doing things you know are wrong because you're trying to obey someone who's leading you down the wrong path. Talk to someone you trust, and they'll help you figure out the best way to handle your situation.

Obeying God is more important than anything else in your life. When you listen carefully to the things He tells you to do, doing your very best to do them quickly, thoroughly, and with a good attitude, things will go well for you!

Bazooka Boys ★ Who Am I?

OBEY STACKING CONTEST

(10 minutes)

Supplies

- Foam pool noodle (1 per team)
- Knife
- Masking tape
- Permanent Marker
- Bag (1 per team)

Prep

- Use the knife to slice the pool noodle into 1 inch disks.
- Place masking tape on each disk and write a word from the them verse with permanent marker: *"Children, obey your parents the way the Lord wants, because this is the right thing to do."* —Ephesians 6:1 (ERV)
- Place all the disks in a bag.

Directions

1. Divide the boys into teams.

2. When you say "go" each boy reaches into the bag and pulls out a disk.

3. Once all the disks have been drawn, the team should work together to stack them in order. (some boys may need to draw twice)

4. First team to stack the verse in the correct order wins!

Bazooka Boys ★ Who Am I?

"DO WHAT I SAY" MAZE CHALLENGE

(20 minutes)

Supplies

- Maze templates
- Blindfolds
- Markers or crayons

Prep

- Copy maze template onto paper (1 of each level of difficulty per boy).

Directions

1. Have each boy find a partner.

2. One boy will be blindfolded, and the other will give directions.

3. When you say "go" the blindfolded boy must follow the instructions of his partner to lead him through the maze.

4. When one boy has completed the maze, they should switch roles.

5. Each boy should take turns with the more challenging mazes until everyone has completed each round.

6. Take a few minutes to discuss how important it was to listen and obey the directions of their partner!

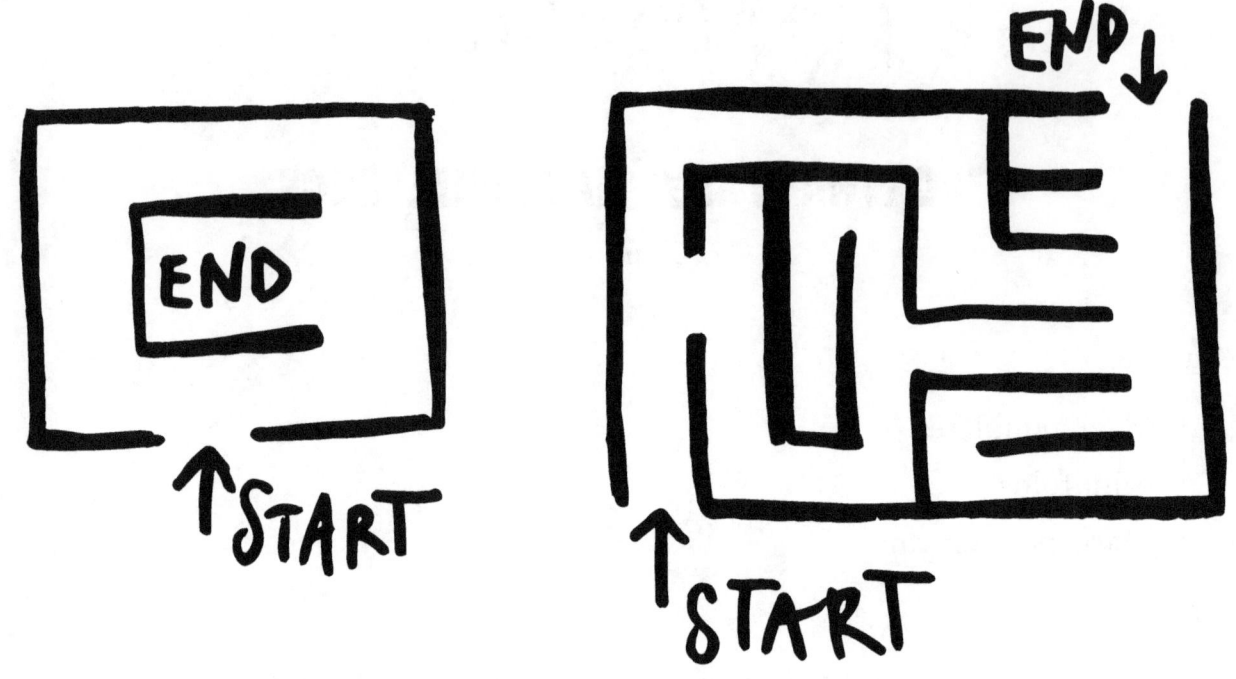
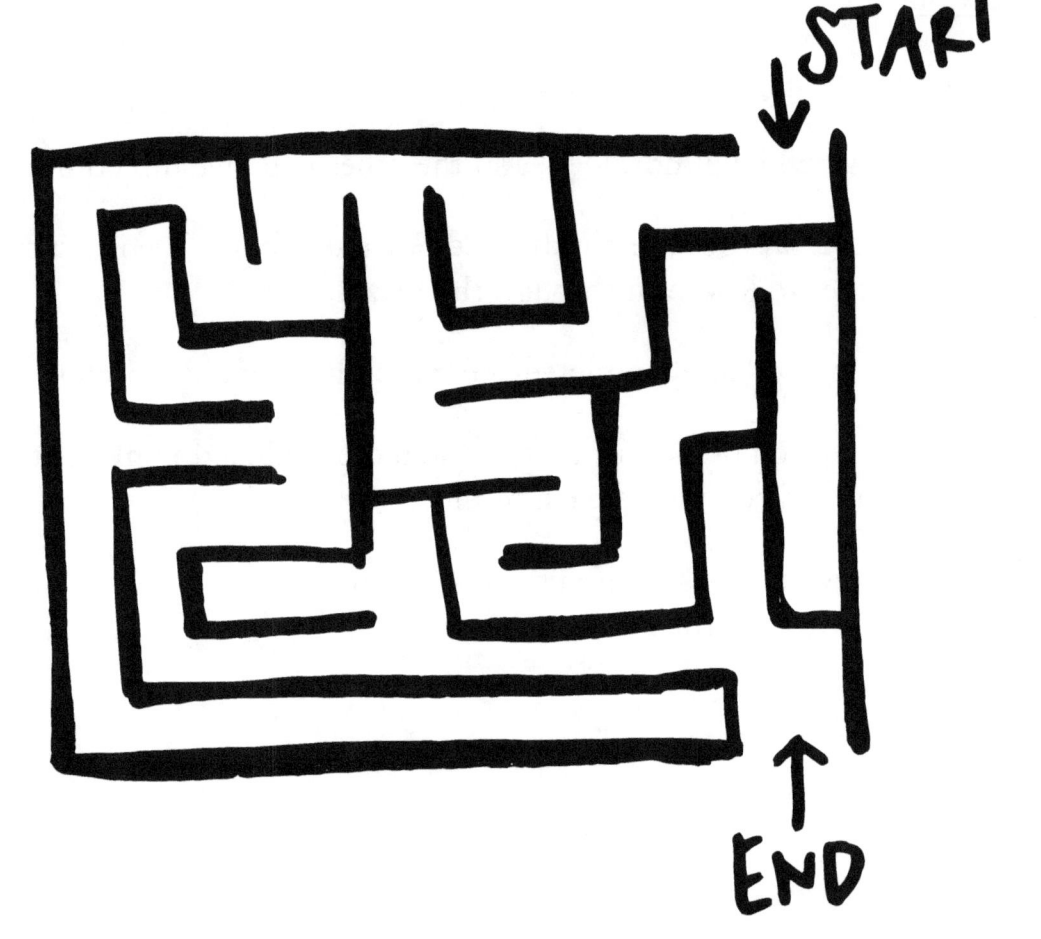

ASK THIS ★ REPEAT THIS ★ PRAY THIS ★ DOODLE THIS
(10 minutes)

Huddle up with your team just before you dismiss.

Ask This:

1. God wants us to obey without delay. Give an example of a time when you didn't obey right away.

2. When we're asked to do something by someone in authority over us, is it okay to only obey part of their instructions? Why is this important?

3. We need to obey with a good attitude. Share a time when you did something you weren't really excited about, but you did it with a good attitude anyway.

Repeat This:

"Children, obey your parents the way the Lord wants, because this is the right thing to do." —Ephesians 6:1 (ERV)

Pray This:

"Dear Jesus, I know that you want me to obey my parents and those in authority. Forgive me for not obeying right away, all the way, and the right way. Help me to do better. Amen."

Doodle This:
Have the boys turn to the Doodle page in their workbook (or copy it for them).

PARENT CONNECTION

Wouldn't it be fantastic if our kids always obeyed us? No procrastinating, no whining, no pretending they've suddenly lost the ability to hear and speak when we ask them to do something. I might actually fall over from shock.

The truth is that obedience doesn't come easily to any of us, especially children. Even if our intentions are to obey, we're often distracted and fail to follow through with what has been asked of us.

This week we talked to the boys about obeying without delay, all the way, the right way. This means that we obey the first time we're asked to do something. We don't wait until it suits us—we obey immediately when someone in authority tells us to do something. Obeying all the way means we do our very best. We complete the task to the best of our abilities. We do it the right way, with a good attitude. No stomping, whining, or complaining allowed!

Our job as parents is to continually prepare our children for the life they will one day encounter outside the walls of our house. One of the most fundamental aspects of a healthy child is their ability to respect and honor what authority has asked them to do. So be patient, be consistent, and keep encouraging them to practice obedience every single day. You won't regret it.

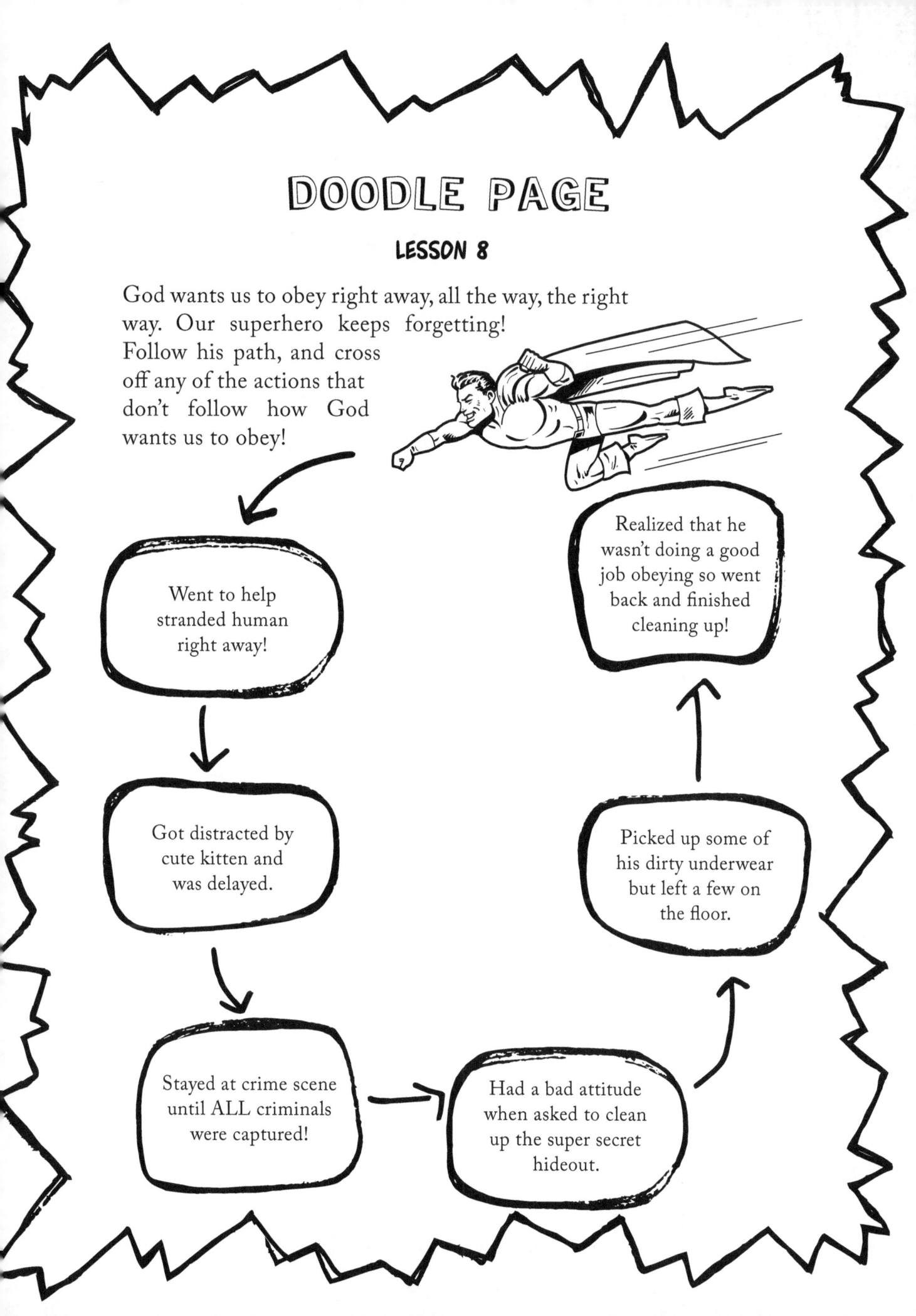

Bazooka Boys ★ Who Am I?

KINDERGARTEN AND 1ST GRADE

Fill in the blanks with the word OBEY.

Ephesians 6:1 (ERV)

Children, _____ your parents the way the Lord wants, because this is the right thing to do.

Jeremiah 42:6 (NLT)

Whether we like it or not, we will _____ the Lord our God to whom we are sending you with our plea. For if we _____ him, everything will turn out well for us.

Psalm 119:60 (NIRV)

I won't waste any time. I will be quick to _____ your commands.

In the squares write:
Complain, whine, cry, yell, stomp

In the circles write:
Ignore, delay, wait, disobey

In the hearts write:
Obey, without, all, right

Color all the circles green.

Color all the squares blue.

Color all the hearts red.

Now fill in the blanks with the words in the hearts:

God wants us to _____, _____ delay,

_____ the way, the _____ way!

Bazooka Boys ★ Who Am I?

When we obey God, we do what He tells us to. We follow the path He wants us to take instead of choosing our own way. Complete the maze below and remind yourself to choose God's path!

Bazooka Boys ★ Who Am I?

2ND AND 3RD GRADE

Fill in the blanks with the word **OBEY**.

Ephesians 6:1 (ERV)

Children, _____ your parents the way the Lord wants, because this is the right thing to do.

Jeremiah 42:6 (NLT)

Whether we like it or not, we will _____ the Lord our God to whom we are sending you with our plea. For if we _____ him, everything will turn out well for us.

Psalm 119:60 (NIRV)

I won't waste any time. I will be quick to _____ your commands.

In the squares write:
Complain, whine, cry, yell, stomp

In the circles write:
Ignore, delay, wait, disobey

In the hearts write:
Obey, without, all, right

Color all the circles green.

Color all the squares blue.

Color all the hearts red.

Now fill in the blanks with the words in the hearts:

God wants us to _____ , _____ delay,

_____ the way, the _____ way!

Bazooka Boys ★ Who Am I?

When we obey God, we do what He tells us to. We follow the path He wants us to take instead of choosing our own way. Complete the maze below and remind yourself to choose God's path!

Bazooka Boys ★ Who Am I?

4TH AND 5TH GRADE

Look up the following verses in your Bible and underline them with a color pencil. Then write them out in the space provided. Write out one way you can follow the truth in your own life in the heart next to each verse.

Ephesians 6:1

Jeremiah 42:6

Psalm 119:60

Do you remember what we learned today? Fill in the blanks.

God wants us to _____ , _____ delay,

_____ the way, the _____ way!

When we obey God, we do what He tells us to. We follow the path He wants us to take instead of choosing our own way. Complete the maze below and remind yourself to choose God's path!

Bazooka Boys ★ Who Am I?

WEEK 8

BAZOOKA BLAST OVERVIEW: WEEK 9

Large Group Lesson: *(15 minutes)*

- Our bodies are God's house, so we need to take care of them!

- We need to make sure we are caring for our bodies by staying clean, brushing our teeth, and exercising!

- We need to only put good things into our bodies…power foods, not lazy foods!

- We can practice self-control with our food choices by remembering **GO**, **SLOW**, and **WHOA** foods!

Bazooka Blitz: Small Group Time:

Bible Blitz *(15 minutes)*
Go, Slow, Whoa Relay *(Instructions on page 223)*

Bazooka Project *(20 minutes)*
Monster Chomp *(Instructions on page 225)*

Team Huddle *(10 minutes)*

Ask This:

1. What does the Bible say about where God lives? (*Answer: Our bodies are God's house!*)

2. What are some ways you can take good care of your body?

3. What are the three kinds of foods we talked about today? Which one do you like to eat the most? What can you do this week to make better food choices?

Repeat This: *"You know that you are God's house. The spirit of God lives in you."* —1 Corinthians 3:16 (WE)

Pray This: *"Dear Jesus, I know that you created my body. Help me to practice self-control by choosing healthy things and taking good care of my body. Amen."*

Doodle This: Turn to the Doodle Page in your workbooks (or copy it for them).

Bazooka Boys ★ Who Am I?

YOUR BODY, GOD'S HOUSE

What's the Point?
Our bodies are God's house, and we need to take good care of His house!

THEME VERSE

You know that you are God's house. The spirit of God lives in you.
1 Corinthians 3:16 (WE)

RELATED BIBLE PASSAGE

Daniel 1:8–19

★ LARGE GROUP LESSON ★
(15 minutes)

What does your house look like? Do you have your own room, or do you share with someone? Did you get to decorate your room a certain way? The place where we live is a very special—it's where we spend time with our family, where we come to rest and relax, where we get away from all the craziness of the world. It's the special place that belongs to us and the people we love.

I don't know about you, but there's nothing I love more than coming home after a long, busy day and walking into my house, where I can smell yummy things cooking and see all the things and people I love. Our homes are important!

Did you know God has a house? It's true—He does! It might surprise you to learn where God's house is. It's not a church or a big mansion. It's actually **YOU**! The Bible tells us the spirit of God lives inside of us in 1 Corinthians 3:16: *"You know that you are God's house. The spirit of God lives in you"* (WE). When we ask Jesus to come into our life, He makes His home inside of us. He lives in us and helps us in every way possible. What a cool thought!

Since God's house is inside our bodies, don't you think it's important for us to take care of our bodies? What would happen to your real house if you never took care of it, if you never took out the trash or cleaned up the dishes? What if you never painted the outside or made sure the grass was mowed? It wouldn't take long before your house would be broken down, messed up, and not very much fun to live in.

Just like we take care of our physical houses, we need to take care of our bodies—God's house!

Bazooka Boys ★ Who Am I?

What are some ways you can take good care of God's house?

 ## 1. TAKE GOOD CARE OF YOUR BODY.

Sam was so excited to **FINALLY** be on summer vacation—no more getting up early to catch the bus, no more homework, no more school lunches! He couldn't wait to just lie around and relax.

He started staying up **WAY** too late every night. He would sneak a flashlight into his room and read his book well into the night. Then he'd sleep in late and stumble down into the kitchen and pour himself a bowl of super-sugary cereal and eat a couple doughnuts. Then he laid on the couch, watching TV for the rest of the morning. He forgot to brush his teeth and decided he'd get to it later. He even forgot to take a shower like his mom told him to do.

By the time dinner rolled around, Sam wasn't feeling so great. His body was **NOT** happy with him. His muscles ached, his tummy hurt, and he felt pretty blah. He realized that, although it sounds fun to be lazy and eat junk all day long, it really made him feel horrible! He decided to go to bed early and try to do better the next day.

God wants you to take good care of your body! That means eating healthy foods, getting plenty of exercise, brushing your teeth every day, and taking baths or showers to make sure that your body stays clean. Taking care of God's house means taking good care of your body!

The second way you can take good care of your bodies is to…

 ## 2. PUT GOOD THINGS INTO YOUR BODY.

Have you ever watched your mom or dad put gas in the car? The gas is the fuel that makes the car work! Your body works the same way—what you put inside it determines how well your body works. Your food is supposed to give your body power.

There are two kinds of food we can put into our bodies: lazy foods and power foods. Lazy foods are full of sugar and fat. They might taste good, but they don't give us any power. Lazy foods include sugary cereals, candy, fast food, and other greasy things.

Power foods fill our bodies with good things that build up our muscles and give us energy. They're filled with vitamins and minerals and protein that give our bodies the fuel they need to work hard. Power foods make your body healthy and strong! Some yummy power foods are fruits, vegetables, nuts, whole grains and lean meat.

When you're choosing the foods you put in your body, choose power foods over lazy foods. Your body will thank you!

The last way you can take good care of your bodies is to…

3. PRACTICE SELF-CONTROL WHEN YOU MAKE YOUR FOOD CHOICES.

I know it seems like a really good idea to eat ten cookies for breakfast, but is that really a good choice? Sometimes we open a bag of candy and just can't seem to help ourselves from eating every last piece right before dinner. It's just so yummy!

One of the biggest areas where we need to practice self-control throughout our lives is what we eat. Your tummy might be screaming loudly, "EAT MORE SUGAR! GIVE ME MORE DONUTS! DON'T EAT THOSE VEGETABLES! GIVE ME POTATO CHIPS INSTEAD!" In that moment, you have to use your self-control to make a better choice to eat things that make your body healthy.

Here's a fun way to help yourself practice self-control with your food—try using the "Go-Slow-Whoa" trick when choosing your food.

GO foods are the very best **POWER** foods—foods that are always a good idea: fruits, veggies, water, and healthy protein like lean meats, yogurt, and nuts.

Choose **GO** foods for most of your daily meals and snacks. Your body will be full of power and energy when you give it this kind of food.

SLOW foods are foods that are good to eat sometimes. They're not really bad for you, but you should only eat them occasionally. They're higher in fat and sugar and have more calories. **SLOW** foods include breads and pastas, cheese, and processed foods. Slow foods still have some nutrition in them, but your diet shouldn't only include **SLOW** foods.

And then there are **WHOA** foods. These are for special occasions. They're high in sugar and fat and don't have much nutritional value. It's okay to have cake or ice cream every once in a while, but if you eat too much too often, your body won't have any energy. If your diet is full of **WHOA** foods, your body won't be working as well as it should be.

Remember, your body is God's house. He made our bodies, and He wants us to take good care of them! Psalm 100:3 says, *"Know that the Lord is God. He made us, and we belong to Him."* When we remember that our bodies belong to God, we'll want to make sure they're as strong and healthy as they can be. This is a great way to show God you're glad He lives inside of you.

Bazooka Boys ★ Who Am I?

GO! SLOW! WHOA! RELAY

(10 minutes)

Supplies

- A variety of food items
  - GO items – fruits and vegetables
  - SLOW items – grains and nuts
  - WHOA items – sweets and treats
- 3 baskets or buckets
- Two tables

Prep

- Set out a variety of food items on two tables, making sure there's the same number of items on each table.
- Include GO foods, WHOA foods, and SLOW Foods.
- Place three baskets or buckets in front of each table.
- Label them with GO, SLOW, and WHOA.

Directions

1. Divide the boys into two teams and line them up on the opposite end of the room.

2. When the game starts, the boys should take turns running to the food table, selecting an item, and dropping it in the appropriate basket.

3. The first team to empty their table wins.

Bazooka Boys ★ Who Am I?

MONSTER CHOMP

(20 minutes)

Supplies

- Plastic Cup (1 per boy)
- White paper
- Pencil
- String
- Tape
- Glue stick
- Broccoli floret (1 per boy)

Prep

- Tie a broccoli floret to a string cut about 18in. long (one for each child)

Directions

1. Trace the open side of the cup onto the paper making a circle.
2. Draw a line through the center of the circle.
3. Draw a zig zag over the center line to create "monster teeth."
4. Cut along the zig zag to create two halves.
5. Glue halves to the rim of the cup, one on top and one on bottom.
6. Tape the string to the inside bottom of the cup with the piece of broccoli hanging down. (Or poke a hole and tie a knot on the outside of the cup)
7. Try to get your monster to eat his broccoli by swinging it and catching it in his mouth.

Bazooka Boys ★ Who Am I?

Ask This:

1. What does the Bible say about where God lives? (*Answer: Our bodies are God's house!*)

2. What are some ways you can take good care of your body?

3. What are the three kinds of foods we talked about today? Which one do you like to eat the most? What can you do this week to make better food choices?

Repeat This:

"You know that you are God's house. The spirit of God lives in you."
—1 Corinthians 3:16 (WE)

Pray This:

Dear Jesus, I know that you created my body. Help me to practice self-control by choosing healthy things and taking good care of my body. Amen.

Doodle This:

Turn to the Doodle Page in your workbook (or copy it for them.)

PARENT CONNECTION

Oh man. This one's gonna be tough. When it comes to teaching our kids self-control in the way they take care of their bodies, we can't just say, "Do as I say, not as I do." If I'm honest, this is one of the greatest areas of struggle in my life, and it can be something I easily brush off and ignore in my parenting.

We want our kids to learn healthy habits and make good decisions **NOW**. We need them to understand the importance of taking good care of their bodies while they're young—it certainly doesn't get easier as they get older!

Today we taught the boys that our bodies are the house God lives in, and we need to take good care of His house! We do this by brushing our teeth, keeping our bodies clean, getting enough rest, etc.

We also taught the boys the difference between foods that give our bodies energy—power foods—and foods that fill our bodies but don't offer anything nutritious—lazy foods. The boys should fill their bodies with power foods that will help them grow big and strong!

We also taught the boys the **GO-SLOW-WHOA** principle. **GO** foods include fruits, vegetables, lean proteins, and dairy. Their diets should consist mostly of these healthy foods. **SLOW** foods include carbs, healthy fats, and other foods that are fine in moderation. **WHOA** foods are the things we should eat sparingly or on special occasions, like ice cream or french fries. I love this concept because it doesn't rule out foods, but it helps the boys recognize what should make up the bulk of their diet.

We all want our kids to be healthy! Teaching them to take care of their bodies is a lifelong skill that they will thank you for later.

Bazooka Boys ★ Who Am I?

DOODLE PAGE

LESSON 9

Draw a picture of **THREE LAZY FOODS** which don't give you energy!

Draw a picture of **THREE POWER FOODS** which make you strong!

Bazooka Boys ★ Who Am I?

KINDERGARDEN AND 1ST GRADE

The Bible says our bodies are God's house. Each one of us has a body that is unique, just the way God made us. Color and decorate this house with your favorite colors and shapes. Make it special, just like you!

We show God we love Him by taking care of the bodies He has given us. Circle the pictures of things that are healthy for our bodies.

Bazooka Boys ★ Who Am I?

# TAKE HOME ACTIVITY

2ST AND 3RD GRADE

The Bible says our bodies are God's house. Each one of us has a body that is unique, just the way God made us. Color and decorate this house with your favorite colors and shapes. Make it special, just like you!

Use the key to solve the word problem below.

1 Corinthians 3:16 (WE)

A	B	C	D	E	F	G	H	I	J	K	L	M	N	O	P	R	S	T	U	V	W	Y
19	9	12	5	21	20	1	17	25	4	3	2	13	16	18	8	10	11	7	14	6	26	22

Y O U **K N O W** **T H A T** **Y O U**
22 18 14   3 16 18 26   7 17 19 7   22 18 14

A R E **G O D** **'** **S** **H O U S E**.
19 10 21   1 18 5   11   17 18 14 11 21

T H E **S P I R I T** **O F** **G O D**
7 17 21   11 8 25 10 25 7   18 20   1 18 5

L I V E S **I N** **Y O U**.
2 25 6 21 11   25 16   22 18 14

We can make healthy choices when it comes to the food we put into our bodies. In the space below, list some things that are **GO** foods, **SLOW** foods, and **WHOA** foods.

GO	SLOW	WHOA

Bazooka Boys ★ Who Am I?

TAKE HOME ACTIVITY

4TH AND 5TH GRADE

Solve the puzzle below to remind yourself where God lives.

1 Corinthians 3:16 (WE)

A	B	C	D	E	F	G	H	I	J	K	L	M	N	O	P	R	S	T	U	V	W	Y
19	9	12	5	21	20	1	17	25	4	3	2	13	16	18	8	10	11	7	14	6	26	22

__ __ __   __ __ __ __   __ __ __ __   __ __ __
22 18 14   3 16 18 26   7 17 19 7   22 18 14

__ __ __   __ __ __ ' __   __ __ __ __ __ .
19 10 21   1 18 5   11   17 18 14 11 21

__ __ __   __ __ __ __ __ __   __ __   __ __ __
7 17 21   11 8 25 10 25 7   18 20   1 18 5

__ __ __ __ __   __ __   __ __ __ .
2 25 6 21 11   25 16   22 18 14

We can make healthy choices when it comes to the food we put into our bodies. In the space below, list some things that are **GO** foods, **SLOW** foods, and **WHOA** foods.

GO	SLOW	WHOA

As we get older, we can sometimes feel bad about how our bodies feel different. It's important to remind yourself that God created your body unique and different on purpose. He wants your body to be healthy, but that doesn't mean every body will look the same. Look up Psalm 139:14 and write it out in the space provided. Then make a list of the ways God made your body unique (things like hair color, eye color, skin color, and any other thing that makes you YOU).

Bazooka Boys ★ Who Am I?

WEEK 9

BAZOOKA BLAST OVERVIEW: WEEK 10

Large Group Lesson: *(15 minutes)*

- We need to practice self-control with our bodies so we don't hurt others with our actions.
- It's important to think before we do something instead of just reacting.
- Our bodies belong to us and other people's bodies belong to them. Respect their personal space.
- We need to keep our bodies under control.

Bazooka Blitz: Small Group Time:

Bible Blitz *(15 minutes)*
Bubble Popping Exercise *(Instructions on page 245)*

Bazooka Project *(20 minutes)*
Sticky Hands *(Instructions on page 247)*

Team Huddle *(10 minutes)*

<u>Ask This:</u>
1. If we're not careful, our bodies can hurt someone else. Name some ways that we can hurt others with our hands. Name some ways we can hurt others with our feet.
2. What are some ways you can respect other people's bodies by controlling your own body? (*Hula hoop, Think about how your actions will make others feel*)
3. Name one way you are going to keep your body under control this week.

<u>Repeat This:</u> "But I discipline my body and keep it under control."
—I Corinthians 9:27

<u>Pray This:</u> "*Dear God, Help me to keep my body under control. I want to use my hands and feet to help others, not hurt others. Amen.*"

<u>Doodle This:</u> Turn to the Doodle Page in your workbooks (or copy it for them).

HANDS AND FEET

WHAT'S THE POINT?
Our bodies belong to God and we need to use them the way He wants us to!

THEME VERSE
But I discipline my body and keep it under control.
1 Corinthians 9:27

RELATED BIBLE PASSAGE
Romans 6:12–14

★ LARGE GROUP LESSON ★

(15 minutes)

Last week we talked about the fact that our bodies are God's house. The Bible says He lives inside of us, so we need to take good care of His house. We should be taking good care of our bodies by exercising, eating good foods, and making sure we stay clean and healthy.

Today we're going to talk more about practicing self-control with our bodies. We need to make sure every part of us is behaving in a way that shows others we belong to God.

Can you think of a time when it seemed like your body was in control of you? Maybe you could **NOT** stay awake during class or church. No matter how hard you tried, your eyes would **NOT** stay open. Your body wanted to sleep, and it seemed like nothing you did kept you awake!

Or maybe you were **REALLY** hungry and your stomach kept growling and growling. No matter how hard you tried **NOT** to, all you could think about was a double cheeseburger with extra bacon and cheese, and your stomach got louder and louder until everyone could hear it.

Or maybe you had to go to the bathroom really, really bad and you just kept jumping and dancing around thinking, "I can wait! I'm having so much fun with my friends. I don't want to stop playing to go inside." Pretty soon you realize that you better go **NOW** because your body is going to take over and you're going to go to the bathroom whether or not you're **IN** the bathroom.

Our bodies can sure be bossy. Sometimes we find ourselves in a situation where we do something with our bodies that we know isn't right. If we wanted to, we could stop ourselves, but we just don't practice self-control.

Have you ever done something with your hands that hurt another person? Maybe you hit your little sister or took something from your neighbor that didn't belong to you. Maybe you wrote something mean about another person or pushed someone because they made you mad.

Have you ever let your feet take you into a situation that you knew wasn't good? Maybe you went over to a friend's house even though you knew your mom had told you not to. Maybe you ran away from a friend who wanted to play with you and hurt his feelings by excluding him. Maybe you stomped your feet in a temper tantrum because you didn't get your way. Or maybe you kicked the door to your bedroom when your mom grounded you for having a bad attitude.

Proverbs 6:18 tells us that God **HATES** "*feet that are quick to do wrong.*" Does that mean that God doesn't like feet? Of course not! It means God doesn't like it when we let our feet take us places that will get us into trouble.

We need to keep our bodies under control. God wants our hands and feet to do good things for Him, not things that could hurt other people or disobey our parents.

What are some things you can do to practice self-control with your body?

You need to...

 **1. tHINK BEFORE YOU ACt.**

Sometimes we do things with our bodies before we stop to think about our actions. Have you ever heard the word "impulsive"? It means you do something before you stop and think.

Instead of reacting in the moment when you're mad or sad or angry, try stopping yourself **BEFORE** you act. Take a deep breath and count to three. Then think about your actions and possible consequences. Are you going to hurt someone? Are you going to make someone sad? Think about how **YOU** would feel if the same thing was done to you, **THEN** make a good choice regarding your actions.

Another smart idea is to ask yourself a few questions before you act. What will happen if you do the thing you're thinking about doing? What will happen if you **DON'T** do the thing you're thinking about doing? Look at both choices and decide which is the better option.

Ephesians 5:17 says, "*Don't act thoughtlessly, but understand what the Lord wants you to do.*" When you act before you think, you're acting thoughtlessly. Stop yourself before you act and ask God if this action will be pleasing to Him. Then make the choice to honor God with your actions.

I know it can be **REALLY** hard to stop yourself when you want to react to something, but it can take just **SECONDS** to say or do something that will have lasting effects on you and others. Don't let your actions happen before you have a chance to think about them. Stop and think. Then act.

The second way we can have self-control with our bodies is to…

 ## 2. RESPECT OTHER PEOPLE'S BODIES.

God gave each one of us a body, and He cares about us! He wants us to care about other people, too. When you do something that hurts or bothers another person, that isn't pleasing to God.

Illustration:

(Have the boys make a circle in front of themselves with their arms out and their fingers connected.)

"This is your hula hoop of personal space. This space belongs to you, and your neighbor's personal space belongs to them.

It's okay for you to ask other people to respect your space. And don't invade your friend or neighbor's personal space without their permission. This is a good way to respect other people's bodies!"

There was a boy in Avery's class who always bothered him. He kicked his chair in class and untied his shoes at recess. Sometimes he would try to distract Avery by making funny noises during quizzes. One day he pushed him down on the playground and he finally had enough.

"You better stop this right now!" he yelled loudly. "You are always in my personal space, and if you don't stop it right now, I'm going to talk to the teacher and make sure you get into trouble." The boy walked away laughing, but Avery felt good that he had stood up for himself.

YOUR BODY BELONGS TO YOU. NO ONE ELSE SHOULD BOTHER YOU, HURT YOU, OR DO THINGS THAT MAKE YOU FEEL UNCOMFORTABLE.

In the same way, you should always respect other people's bodies. Be kind and careful when you're playing games. Don't push or shove others. Don't distract others by poking them, throwing things, or doing anything else that could keep them from doing their best when they're trying to concentrate.

Philippians 2:3 says, *"In whatever you do, don't let selfishness or pride be your guide. Be humble, and honor others more than yourselves"* (ERV). God wants you to care about other people, and that includes respecting their bodies.

The last way you can practice self-control with your body is to…

3. KEEP YOUR BODY UNDER CONTROL.

It's not easy to keep your body under control, but that is exactly what you need to do every single day. First Corinthians 9:27 says, *"But I discipline my body and keep it under control."* God wants us to be in charge of what our bodies do. This means practicing self-control instead of letting our bodies do whatever comes to mind.

You can practice self-control with your body when you choose NOT to hit someone when you get angry with them. You can practice self-control when you refuse to throw a tantrum even though you're disappointed that your parents won't let you do something. You can practice self-control when you respond to your sister with a calm, quiet voice instead of yelling at her. You can practice self-control with your body by sitting still when the teacher has asked you not to get up from your desk. None of these things are easy, but you can do them! God has promised to help you practice self-control. If you pray and ask God for His help, He has promised to give you the strength to be disciplined with your actions.

BUBBLE POPPING EXERCISE

(10 minutes)

Supplies

- Bubbles

Directions

1. You can either have a few volunteers come forward for this exercise, or if your group is small, do it with the whole group.

2. Take a bottle of bubbles and tell the kids you're going to blow bubbles at them.

3. Their job is to remain perfectly still and not catch, stomp, pop, or doing anything else to the bubbles.

4. If someone moves, they are out.

5. Last boy left is the winner!

6. This is a great example of what it means to practice self-control with their bodies!

Bazooka Boys ★ Who Am I?

STICKY HANDS

(20 minutes)

<u>Supplies</u>

- Sticky Hands toy (gel party favors with stretchy string)
- Index cards
- Tape
- Crayons/markers/colored pencils

<u>Prep</u>

- Purchase sticky hand toy (one per child)
- Designate an area on the wall for the index cards to be posted.
- Make a tape line on the floor to stay behind.

<u>Directions</u>

1. Give each boy four index cards.
2. On each card, have the boy write an action (Two with actions that are good, and two that are bad.)
3. Tape the cards onto a wall.
4. Have the boys throw their sticky hands towards the cards on the wall.
5. If a hand sticks to a card, have the boy read it out loud. If it's a positive action, repost it to the wall. If it's a negative action, crumple it up and throw it away.
6. Keep throwing the hands until all the bad cards are in the trash.

Bazooka Boys ★ Who Am I?

WEEK 10

Ask This:

1. If we're not careful, our bodies can hurt someone else. Name some ways that we can hurt others with our hands. Name some ways we can hurt others with our feet.

2. What are some ways you can respect other people's bodies by controlling your own body? (*Hula hoop, Think about how your actions will make others feel*)

3. Name one way you are going to keep your body under control this week.

Repeat This:

"But I discipline my body and keep it under control." —I Corinthians 9:27

Pray This:

"Dear God, Help me to keep my body under control. I want to use my hands and feet to help others, not hurt others. Amen."

Doodle This:

Turn to the Doodle Page in your workbook (or copy it for them.)

PARENT CONNECTION

I'm sure I'm not the only parent who has said, "Keep your hands to yourself!" a million times. Kids are busy and impulsive, and if they're not careful, their hands and feet can get them into trouble!

We're all impulsive to some extent, but one of the greatest lessons we must learn as we're growing up is to control our compulsions and discipline our actions. This week we talked to the boys about controlling their hands and feet. This involves the actions of their hands and feet, as well as being careful about where their feet are taking them.

We reminded them that they should stop and think before they act. They may need to take a few deep breaths or count to three before they respond. We encouraged them to think through the consequences of their actions BEFORE they act. If they can give themselves a minute to calm down and process the ramifications of their behavior, the chances of them making a good choice go up significantly.

Then we talked about respecting other people's bodies. This includes not hitting, kicking, or distracting others as well as honoring their personal space.

We also taught the boys to practice controlling their bodies instead of simply reacting and doing whatever comes to them compulsively. Intentionally keeping our bodies under control is something we all need to do.

It may take some time, but if your son will put in the practice, he can become disciplined with his hands and feet!

DOODLE PAGE

LESSON 10

We can use our hands to help others or to hurt others. On the handprints below, write out some ways you can help others with your hands! Then in the space provided, draw a picture of yourself doing one of those things!

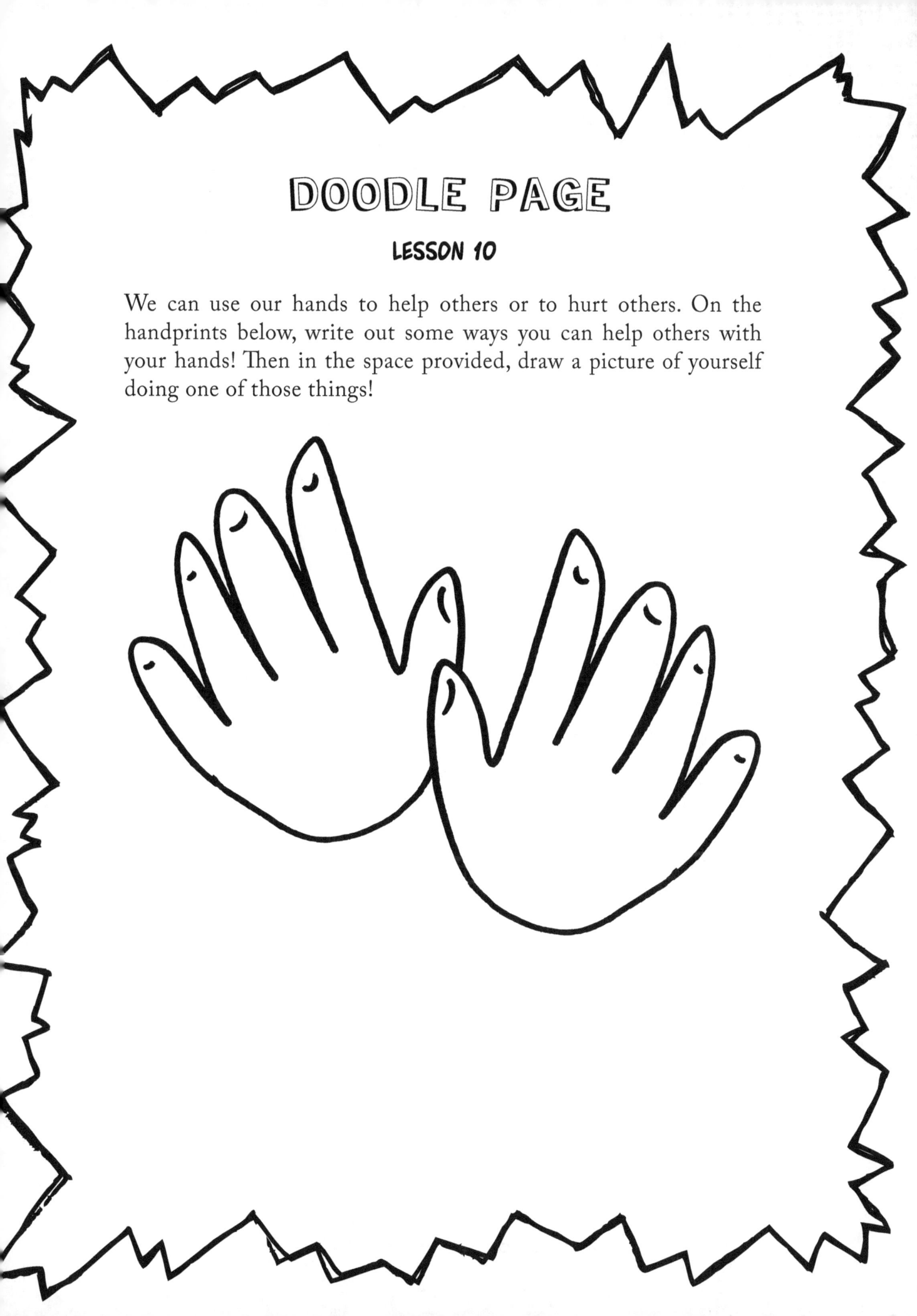

Bazooka Boys ★ Who Am I?

KINDERGARDEN AND 1ST GRADE

Write the word **BODY** in the blank spaces below.

But don't let sin control your life here on earth. You must not be ruled by the things your sinful self makes you want to do. Don't offer the parts of your _____ to serve sin. Don't use your _____ to do evil, but offer yourselves to God, as people who have died and now live. Offer the parts of your _____ to God to be used for doing good. – Romans 6:12–13 (ERV)

Today we learned that we should think before we act. In the scenarios below, circle the **RIGHT** way to act in each situation.

1. Someone takes your toy:

    a. Hitting back   b. Asking for toy back

2. Your sister is being annoying:

    a. Kick your sister   b. Walk away

3. You don't get the candy you want at the store:

    a. Throw a tantrum   b. Be sad but accept it

4. You lose at softball:

    a. Cry "It's not fair, you cheated!"   b. Shake hands with other team and say "Good job"

We need to respect other people's bodies and personal space. Philippians 2:3 says, "*In whatever you do, don't let selfishness or pride be your guide. Be humble, and honor others more than yourselves*" (ERV).

Find the hidden words below.

R	I	H	X	E	A	R	E
V	P	O	C	N	T	M	L
D	G	M	X	E	M	O	B
S	D	H	D	Y	K	P	M
G	Z	I	M	A	L	O	U
X	R	H	O	N	O	R	H
P	S	V	H	F	H	P	L
H	P	M	X	E	S	D	G

Word List:

Humble

Honor

Pride

Bazooka Boys ★ Who Am I?

2ND AND 3RD GRADE

Some key words are missing in the verse beliw. Using the first letter of the word as a clue, fill in the missing words using the key below.

But don't let sin C_____ your life here on earth. You must not be ruled by the things your S_____ self makes you want to do. Don't offer the parts of your B_____ to serve sin. Don't use your B_____ to do evil, but offer Y_____ to God, as people who have died and now live. Offer the parts of your B_____ to God to be used for doing G_____.

– Romans 6:12–13 (ERV)

Word List

Good	*Yourselves*	*Sinful*
Body	*Control*	

Today we learned that we should think before we act. In the scenarios below, circle the **RIGHT** way to act in each situation.

1. Someone takes your toy:
    a. Hitting back
    b. Asking for toy back

2. Your sister is being annoying:
    a. Kick your sister
    b. Walk away

3. You don't get the candy you want at the store:
    a. Throw a tantrum
    b. Be sad but accept it

4. You lose at softball:
    a. Cry "It's not fair, you cheated!"
    b. Shake hands with other team and say "Good job"

We need to respect other people's bodies and personal space. Philippians 2:3 says, "*In whatever you do, don't let selfishness or pride be your guide. Be humble, and honor others more than yourselves*" (ERV).

Find the hidden words below.

```
I O V H R Q E P M W D C D Q O
P Q I O Z O K T M T U K D G C
L E D I R P N N W B J R W B U
K C M I F G H O C P I U Z K A
R M N X N H V Z H H G D Z X X
Y L H A U E P X Z Q U C G H T
S E L M P C V E U F U Q P O R
U U B Q S A F G R H O O P I E
H L S E P P P A C S R J Y U S
E H N Z P S F X M J O M X J P
A Q B H N R T Y O V Q N P D E
V T Z V J L J T T Z U L A Y C
X U S E L F I S H N E S S L T
E R I E M X O Z W P B Y X R L
D M C D N F K T H K M A W V J
```

Word List:

Honor	Hoop	Hula
Humble	Personal	Pride
Respect	Selfishness	Space

Bazooka Boys ★ Who Am I?

TAKE HOME ACTIVITY

4TH AND 5TH GRADE

Look up Romans 6:12–13 in your Bible and write it in the space provided.

Today we learned we need to think before we act. For each scenario below, write out the wrong way to react and the right way to act.

1. Someone steals your spot in line.

2. Your sister is driving you crazy and you just want her to leave you alone.

3. Your friend didn't invite you to her party and your feelings are hurt.

4. You lose the championship game and you're really upset.

5. Your brother takes the last Fruit Roll-Up and he KNEW you wanted it.

Bazooka Boys ★ Who Am I?

We need to respect other people's bodies and personal space. Philippians 2:3 says, *"In whatever you do, don't let selfishness or pride be your guide. Be humble, and honor others more than yourselves"* (ERV).

Find the hidden words below.

```
I O V H R Q E P M W D C D Q O
P Q I O Z O K T M T U K D G C
L E D I R P N N W B J R W B U
K C M I F G H O C P I U Z K A
R M N X N H V Z H H G D Z X X
Y L H A U E P X Z Q U C G H T
S E L M P C V E U F U Q P O R
U U B Q S A F G R H O O P I E
H L S E P P P A C S R J Y U S
E H N Z P S F X M J O M X J P
A Q B H N R T Y O V Q N P D E
V T Z V J L J T T Z U L A Y C
X U S E L F I S H N E S S L T
E R I E M X O Z W P B Y X R L
D M C D N F K T H K M A W V J
```

Word List:

Honor	*Hoop*	*Hula*
Humble	*Personal*	*Pride*
Respect	*Selfishness*	*Space*

www.ingramcontent.com/pod-product-compliance
Lightning Source LLC
Chambersburg PA
CBHW060418010526
44118CB00017B/2272